T0360433

Sales Management

Sales are the lifeblood of the business world and therefore an area of fundamental importance for scholarly research. This concise book analyses current thoughts and emerging practices in sales management research.

Organisations that are looking to increase revenues and add new customers to their portfolio will find it increasingly difficult to successfully do this without being aware of and adopting the appropriate, adaptive sales processes. Emergent themes such as agile sales management, digital selling, artificial intelligence and trust will be discussed in the book that also embraces the importance of customer relationship management, and how salespeople are aligning their interactions with the marketing function. The text will review recent research to identify how to grow and organise the sales pipeline, manage hybrid sales teams, and the effects of new technologies on selling processes. These discussions will be helpful in highlighting issues and providing some solutions to practitioners who are operating in new environments.

This book will be invaluable to sales researchers as it summarises current knowledge about key sales and sales management topics and indicates possible future research directions.

Kenneth Le Meunier-FitzHugh is an Associate Professor in Marketing at the University of East Anglia, UK.

Kieran Sheahan is a Lecturer at Technological University, Dublin, Ireland.

State of the Art in Business Research
Series Editor: Geoffrey Wood

Recent advances in theory, methods and applied knowledge (alongside structural changes in the global economic ecosystem) have presented researchers with challenges in seeking to stay abreast of their fields and navigate new scholarly terrains.

State of the Art in Business Research presents short-form books that provide an expert map to guide readers through new and rapidly evolving areas of research. Each title will provide an overview of the area, a guide to the key literature and theories and time-saving summaries of how theory interacts with practice.

As a collection, these books provide a library of theoretical and conceptual insights, and exposure to novel research tools and applied knowledge, that aid and facilitate in defining the state of the art, as a foundation stone for a new generation of research.

Cultural Management
A Research Overview
Chris Bilton

Ethical Consumption
A Research Overview
Alex Hiller and Helen Goworek

Strategic Human Resource Management, 2e
A Research Overview
John Storey and Patrick M. Wright

Sales Management
A Research Overview
Kenneth Le Meunier-FitzHugh and Kieran Sheahan

For more information about this series, please visit: www.routledge.com/State-of-the-Art-in-Business-Research/book-series/START

Sales Management
A Research Overview

**Kenneth Le Meunier-FitzHugh
and Kieran Sheahan**

LONDON AND NEW YORK

First published 2023
by Routledge
4 Park Square, Milton Park, Abingdon, Oxon OX14 4RN

and by Routledge
605 Third Avenue, New York, NY 10158

Routledge is an imprint of the Taylor & Francis Group, an informa business

© 2023 Kenneth Le Meunier-FitzHugh and Kieran Sheahan

The right of Kenneth Le Meunier-FitzHugh and Kieran Sheahan to be identified as authors of this work has been asserted in accordance with sections 77 and 78 of the Copyright, Designs and Patents Act 1988.

British Library Cataloguing-in-Publication Data
A catalogue record for this book is available from the British Library

Library of Congress Cataloguing-in-Publication Data
Names: Le Meunier-FitzHugh, Kenneth, author. | Sheahan, Kieran, 1959- author.
Title: Sales management : a research overview / Kenneth Le Meunier-FitzHugh and Kieran Sheahan.
Description: 1 Edition. | New York : Routledge, 2023. | Series: State of the art in business research | Includes bibliographical references and index.
Identifiers: LCCN 2023011181 (print) | LCCN 2023011182 (ebook) | ISBN 9781032003825 (hardback) | ISBN 9781032555997 (paperback) | ISBN 9781003173892 (ebook)
Subjects: LCSH: Sales management.
Classification: LCC HF5438.4 .L4 2023 (print) | LCC HF5438.4 (ebook) | DDC 658.8/1--dc23/eng/20230331
LC record available at https://lccn.loc.gov/2023011181
LC ebook record available at https://lccn.loc.gov/2023011182

ISBN: 978-1-032-00382-5 (hbk)
ISBN: 978-1-032-55599-7 (pbk)
ISBN: 978-1-003-17389-2 (ebk)

DOI: 10.4324/9781003173892

Typeset in Times New Roman
by MPS Limited, Dehradun

To my mother, Margaret Roy (1931-2023) who died just as this book was completed.

-Ken

To my wife Mary and my children, Mark, KJ, Aisling, Maria Christina, Emma Jayne, thank you for always being there supporting me on my journey

-Kieran

Contents

List of Figures and Tables

Figures

Table

Preface

Sales is the lifeblood of businesses and consequently a driver of both national and global economies. A Professor once asked his students to name the number one reason for why businesses fail. The students highlighted a range of issues from bad management, poor products, cash-flow problems and lack of marketing as being the main reasons that businesses fail. Having reviewed all the answers, the Professor stood in front of the class and wrote three words on the board, 'lack of sales'. Consequently, companies looking to increase revenues and add new customers will find it difficult to successfully do this without the appropriate, adaptive sales processes.

New trends are emerging that are challenging organisations as they strive to achieve sales excellence. They include longer sales cycles, the emergence of virtual selling environments (including inside sales) and AI, new customer relationships, and an increase in the importance of customer insights. Academic research in sales is providing evidence and guidance around these topics. This text will consider emerging areas in sales research, including customer relationships, sales and its relationship with marketing, managing the sales pipeline, sales leadership and the effects of new technologies on selling. We will consider evidence from theory and practice around the need for salespeople to maintain and build personal trust and rapport with their customers within an increasingly virtual sales environment. Organisations and salespeople need to attract and retain customers, but they are trying to balance face-to-face interactions with the necessity of improving their online interactions. This book will explore some of the new avenues of research and practice that will be needed in the future to understand the changing nature of sales at the beginning of the 21st century.

About the Authors

Kenneth Le Meunier-FitzHugh holds a PhD from the University of Warwick in Marketing and Strategic Management, and he is currently an Associate Professor in Marketing at the University of East Anglia. Ken has lectured at the London School of Economics, Cranfield School of Management, King's College London, and St Andrews University. Prior to that he spent 20 years working in senior roles in a range of organisations including Yamaha and Thorn/EMI. Based on these experiences his research focusses on improving the interface between sales and marketing, for which he has an international reputation. Ken has a published a number of articles in key academic journals, including the *Journal of Business Research, Journal of Industrial Marketing Management, European Journal of Marketing and Journal of Personal Selling and Sales Management*. He has also published several noted books, including *Achieving a Strategic Sales Focus: Contemporary issues and Future Challenges, Marketing, A Very Short Introduction* and co-edited *The Oxford Handbook of Strategic Sales and Sales Management*, all for Oxford University Press. Ken has recently revised a bestselling textbook, *Selling and Sales Management*.

Kieran Sheahan is currently Lecturer at TU Dublin and has over 30 years industry experience. He has worked in procurement managing significant contracts within the global supply chain. After achieving international experience in procurement this prompted him to create an enterprise as a co-founder with the key focus driving global sales and profits. He transitioned successfully into sales and their enterprise worked with European/North American/Asian companies helping them drive their European sales in various industries. He has opened up sales channels in the main European markets along with extending his reach to Ukraine, China and South America. He has established strategic partnerships for companies and set up JV's in China and North America. He is strong in talent spotting and developing salespeople as high value and high performers. He has good leadership skills and strongly believes in developing colleagues in the team to create leaders. He has successfully implemented global sales systems and sales processes in order to align global expectations with local market realities. He joined Academia in 2019 lecturing in sales and completed his PhD in 2020, which was focussed on the front end of the sales process-sales pipeline management.

1 Challenges and Changes in Sales

Introduction

The objective of the chapter is to highlight some of the current issues that are affecting sales activities in organisations. We will consider how technology and the pandemic have changed how organisations are managing sales relationships, but more importantly how this is affecting the template of how business will be conducted in the future. We will therefore consider the role of sales in organisations today and explore why research into sales practice is becoming increasingly important to all organisations, whether they are selling consumer or industrial products. We will highlight the environmental and technical challenges that are producing the latest thinking in sales research. We will also explore some of the key changes to sales practice that the discipline is facing such as adaptive sales management, changing customer demands, advances in sales technology, agility and the development of virtual selling environments, which are forcing sales operations to adapt to survive. There are significant streams of literature developing on key issues and challenges in sales processes and sales management, such as customer acquisition and customer relationship management, sales and marketing cooperation, sales management and customer relationship management (CRM) and the role of sales automation technology and social media in sales processes and these streams of literature are going to be discussed throughout this text.

Challenges and Changes in Sales

Sales are at the centre of businesses processes and as Peter Drucker articulated in 1986, the purpose of a business is to create a customer and everybody within the company should be involved in helping to create sales. You can have the best products, wonderful premises and great staff, but these are just costs that need to be offset by revenue generated by the sales team (Drucker, 1986). There is a distinction in sales literature between business-to-consumer (B2C) and business-to-business

DOI: 10.4324/9781003173892-1

(B2B) markets that affects the processes that the prospective purchaser goes through when making a buying decision. Consumer markets are generally serviced through a combination of direct (telesales, mail order and websites) and indirect sales interactions (both online and offline retail outlets and platforms) that address the need for personalised purchases. While B2B sales, whether they are for consumer goods or industrial products to other businesses, are more likely to involve selling through the buyer/sales interface. In this B2B arena, traditionally personal selling is often more cost effective than employing other forms of marketing as the buyer is purchasing on behalf of their business or for resale, but this has been changing in recent times.

Sales, over the past 20 years, has been emerging as an academic discipline, rather than as a subset of marketing. Although the sales function has always been discussed in books such as 'How to win friends and influence people' by Dale Carnegie from 1936, it has only been in the past 20 years that academic rigour around sales has been developed, through the efforts of writers such as Michael Ahearne, Karen Flaherty, Paolo Guenzi, Mark Johnston, Kenneth Le Meunier-FitzHugh, Greg Marshall, Bill Moncrief, Robert Palmatier, Nigel Piercy, Adam Rapp, and Andy Zoltners. Sales as a discipline has struggled to gain the respect it has earned from business leaders, even if it is the foundation of the business's revenue and drives most economies (Moncrief, 2017). However, customers and buyers are facing four clear challenges, (A) a rapidly changing landscape, (B) increasingly sophisticated sellers, (C) the impact of new technology and (D) growth in emerging markets (Grewar et al., 2015).

The sales function is also transforming, and sales is playing an increasingly important role in creating strategic competitive advantage for the organisation as it meets the needs of the new landscape, with customers and consumers demanding higher value propositions and customised solutions within dynamic markets driven by social media communications and changing sales technologies (Cuevas, 2017; Guenzi, Sajtos and Troilo, 2016). In a study of possible future directions of research in selling and sales management Rapp and Beeler (2021) identified that the sales leadership needs to be focused on developing adaptive sales teams that can deliver the required sales strategies to attract and keep new customers, and that salespeople need to develop new individual skill sets that respond to the challenges created by new sales technologies. These themes will be developed over the next few chapters.

The Sales Role

The discussion on how sales practices have evolved into the 21st century covers a wider range of activities between buyers and sellers, such as relationship marketing, solution selling, spin selling and managing the customer journey (Arli, Bauer and Palmatier, 2018; Borg and Young, 2014; Moncrief, 2017). Of the many roles that a salesperson fulfils, customer acquisition and customer retention are possibly the most important. Person-to-person interactions are powerful tools that affect human psychology cannot be ignored (Rapp and Beeler, 2021). Excellent salespeople are not only able to make an initial sale to a new customer but are then able to build long-lasting relationships with them leading to repeat sales, referrals and brand loyalty. Identifying the skills required by the sales role is therefore critical to the success of the business. Salespeople need to have strong time management skills as they can spend more than 60% of their time on administrative tasks, travelling to customers and waiting to speak with their buyers, so they need to use the available time (on or off-line) in front of the buyer carefully (Krogue, 2018). They also need to be good communicators and should always be one step ahead of the customer ready with relevant information and market insights. While being fully aware of the qualities and functionality of the product/service being offered is taken for granted the previous information asymmetry between organisations and customers no longer exists because, in the age of social media, customers are perfectly capable of finding the information they need through a web page, a blog or even YouTube, leading to a situation where they don't need basic information from the salesperson (Marshall et al., 2012).

The seven steps of selling, which is the oldest paradigm in the sales discipline, have been cited in numerous articles (see Figure 1.1), but Moncrief and Marshall (2005) proposed that the traditional seven steps model needed additional nuances to adapt it to the modern selling environment. Additional sales activities such as knowledge management, nurturing customers, problem-solving, adding value/satisfying needs, maintaining customer relationships have been proposed as shaping the new buyer/sales relationship (Castro-González and Bande, 2019). Technological developments are transforming both the front end of the sales process (such as customer acquisition) and the back end of the sales process around relationship selling. The development of relationship selling is highlighting key challenges that are facing salespeople, for example, how to move from the initial call or contact to taking an order, at the same time as establishing trust and the foundation for a longer-term relationship with the buyers. It is important to recognise the customer/buyers in B2B relationships aim to purchase the desired products at the best price. With the rapid changes taking place in the business sphere, sales organisations need to adapt at a very fast rate, and sales research may be lagging in some cases (Arli, Bauer and Palmatier, 2018).

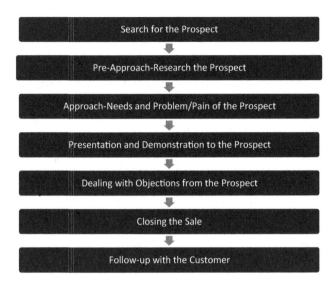

Figure 1.1 The Seven Steps of Selling.
Source: Adapted from Dubinsky, 1981.

Keeping Customers

A key objective in sales strategy is to market a solution to identified customers' problems so that whatever the inconvenience is that a customer may have can be remedied, which calls for a consultative selling approach where the salesperson behaves more like an advisor than a traditional product salesperson (Bean, 2022). Salespeople also need to have empathy with their customers in addition to their professional selling abilities. Whether they are dealing with companies or consumers, they are ultimately speaking to human beings, so a distinctive personality can facilitate bringing people closer together, which in turn can lead to closing sales. Knight (2017) suggests that putting yourself in your counterpart's shoes is essential in a sales situation. Several descriptions have been applied to this facility, including the ability to listen with sincerity and understand the customers' needs and problems, as well as problem solving, cognitive skill, emotional intelligence and confidence (Negley, 2022). Salespeople must realise customers have needs and pain points, as well as rational and emotional issues that influence their buying behaviours. This combination of these competencies forms the bases of the salespersons' ability to gain the trust of the buyer. The salesperson serves as a conduit through which they can influence buyer's decisions through adaptive selling and passion for service and trust (Hartmann et al., 2020).

Salespeople are encouraged to maintain their relationships with existing customers and constantly update them about new products. This means that the salesperson has a dual role as the vendor of new products to customers as well as the provider of insights of customers' needs to the marketing team. From an internal perspective, the salesperson is often the best source of customer and competitor information, as existing customers provide new and innovative ideas to the organisation, which are invaluable. They can compare their organisation's offering with that of their competitors and the markets, building social intelligence and promoting organisational learning (Flaherty et al., 2012). Salespeople also need to record feedback of the customers and address grievances if they have any.

Externally, salespeople are being asked to engage in conversations with customers, understand their needs and develop long-term relationships that provide lifetime value to the sales organisation. At present, everything revolves around customers, including the concepts of customer value and customisation. Creating a value proposition is challenging as buyers are demanding more from their suppliers and value creation is embedded with the interactions between the buying organisation and the seller (Cuevas, 2018). A report in 2020 from the Rain Group identified from a survey of 528 global buyers that they preferred salespeople that were able to demonstrate concern and understanding of their worries and needs when making their purchase decisions. These traits that were appreciated were the ability to provide solutions, value creation opportunities by listening and making clear Return on Investment-based case for the purchase (The Rain Group, 2020).

In the Business-to-Business (B2B) market, salespeople must be able to identify the key participants in the sale and be able to craft their sales pitch to the decision-makers in the buying team who have the power to approve the purchase. It is also important that suitable sales negotiation tactics are used to attract prospective purchasers. It is unavoidable that customers will take longer periods to decide to purchase when it comes to large or expensive orders, but a high-pressure sales tactic may push them to make a hasty decision that they later regret, or they may even walk away from the negotiation. Conversely, using a soft-selling approach may not be persuasive enough to convince the buyer of the value of the product. Therefore, it is essential that salespeople should thoroughly consider and choose the proper technique to present products and services, based on the types of products, and the types of customers (Henshall, 2019). Repeated interactions instil confidence in the customer or client and gives them the opportunity to ask questions and provide feedback. Therefore, salespeople must have good relations with employees and managers of the buying organisation at all levels.

Developments in Sales Technology

Today, it is necessary for a salesperson to be proficient with technology as most sales are acquired, processed and assessed through technological means. Skilled use of sales technology tools can enable salespeople to save on travelling costs, analyse customer behaviour, reduce the time taken up by administrative tasks and improve their offer. The disadvantage of new technology tools will require salespeople to learn how to use these technologies effectively, which may be time consuming (Krogue, 2018), so any salesperson that is not proficient in the use of sales technology and software will need to be trained. The Covid pandemic has accelerated the process of digital transformation including in sales. B2B sales was seen as something that was difficult to do online, but when marketplaces were closed environments due to the pandemic, organisations and customers were forced to buy and sell products online. Consequently, their effectiveness of reaching and serving a customer improved, increasing online in sales, and strengthening processes. While the internet allows salespeople to engage with customers through social media, rather than face-to-face communication, but it should be noted that this may not be as effective for complex products (Corsaro and D'Amico, 2022) and salespeople will need to make this call. B2B sales now include a new range of sales processes such as omnichannel sales, inside sales, technology-based sales and e-commerce, and these developments are set to be long-lasting.

How buyers and sellers communicate with each other has changed and new approaches have had to be implemented in working and closing out tasks (Hartmanna Lussier, 2020). Prior to the pandemic, research identified how companies were making the transition to digital transformation (Guenzi and Habel, 2020; Syam and Sharma, 2018). However, the Covid-19 Pandemic accelerated this process significantly and sales departments were forced to adapt rapidly to the changing landscape and proceed to a remote working model (Rangarajan et al., 2021). Using technology, companies moved very quickly to adapt to these changes with a high percentage of salespeople working remotely with prospects and customers via videoconferencing through platforms such as Teams or Zoom, or by phone. Almost overnight companies had to build more *inside* sales teams as salespeople could no longer meet face-to-face with buyers due to quarantine rules restricting people's movements (Sheahan, 2020).

An inside-sales team supports field sales and interacts with customers and prospects virtually dealing with customer enquiries including offering product and technical assistance (Sleep et al., 2020). Where sellers lack the opportunity to meet with customers face-to-face, they should routinely rely on remote communication to interact with customers. Moreover, buyers are changing their preferences from face-to-face interactions to virtual-based relationships, leading to a future full of opportunities for salespeople using social media. While an inside-sales team can contribute towards reducing costs and deal with outside sales support issues, it may lead to a decrease in the development of the customer relationship unless they use technology and business intelligence tools to enable this process (Rapp et al., 2012; Webb and Hogan, 2002). It is worth noting the sales growth that is taking place in relation to 'inside-sales' and companies need to be aware of this. During this period almost 90% of sales have moved to a videoconferencing (VC)/phone/web sales model, and while some scepticism remains, more than half of salespeople believe this is equally or more effective than sales models used before the pandemic. Out of 3600 B2B Decision Maker's surveyed Globally (Ryan et al., 2020):

- 96% of their Sales Forces have been moved to a remote model
- 65% say the remote model is 'Just as' effective
- We are twice as likely to win business if our Digital offering is exceptional
- 4/5 state that the remote offering will remain post COVID-19

It is recommended that sales leaders should review the most appropriate tools for their business and identify which ones they could implement in their company (Moore et al., 2015). The researched identified LinkedIn as one of the most effective social media platforms to use in sales and marketing. Sales management needs to help sales teams demonstrate to the customers their true value contributions as it can help give them a sustainable advantage (Jaakkola, Frosen and Tikkaned, 2015). Salespeople need to approach customers with a more consultative mindset with solution selling being a core sales capability (Ryan et al., 2020).

Research has highlighted that building trust (Kaski et al., 2017) with the prospects and customers are critical and without this trust, no business or partnerships would take place. Trust and commitment are key elements in achieving relationship benefits with the customer with the added dimension of seeking this early at the front end of the sales process (Arli, Bauer and Palmatier, 2018). All participants felt that it was important to build up trust early with the prospect and to respond quickly to any requests they have (Salomonson, Aberg and Allwood, 2012). The issue of persistence and building trust fits well with the relationship aspect of B2B sales that is prevalent in the literature (Hughes, 2013; Wagner and Mai, 2015). Integrity also came across from the research as important especially when making commitments to the customers. These concepts will be explored further in Chapter 2.

Acquiring New Customers

Identifying potential clients and generating new customer leads is crucial to generating new sales. Salespeople can look for potential customers through a range of media such as cold calling through emails, letters or in person, interacting on social media, website interactions and placing advertisements in suitable places (Rapp and Beeler, 2021). Of course, a variety of social media sites may be used to interact with prospects and customers, but research has identified LinkedIn as the most successful social media prospecting technology tool in searching for new prospects and collecting intelligence on them before they make contact (Sheahan, 2020). LinkedIn is seen as an excellent tool for several reasons, including the ability to check out a prospect before making contact, generating quality leads by matching them against their customer profile, promoting their offer and tracking where their network has moved to when they change companies so that they can approach them and win new customers.

In some organisations the sales pipeline is referred to as the sales funnel, where customers who are 'ready to buy' are identified by being processed down the pipeline (Yu and Cai, 2007). This sales pipeline starts at the top where initial opportunities are reviewed. Where appropriate these are moved to qualified leads and some of them become warm leads. The warm leads are converted into qualified leads so that sales proposals can be formulated, and finally some of these proposals convert into actual new customers. During the pre-approach and approach stages salespeople can look at a potential customer's Web page to learn about their needs so that they can adjust their approach and presentation (see Figure 1.2).

Figure 1.2 The Sales Pipeline Activities.
Source: Created by Sheahan, 2020.

Nurturing leads is the behaviour where salespeople move potential customers from 'cold to warm' which leads to a greater chance of converting the lead into a sale (Jarvinen and Taiminen, 2015). It is very important to have a qualified pipeline management system in place (Hughes, 2013). The pipeline can help determine what opportunities exist and what needs to be done to convert them into sales. It is essential when the lead is being qualified that the organisation has the resources to deliver the products to meet the agreed deadlines of the customer. This will ensure there are no issues later with dissatisfied customers.

Poor sales revenue can be attributed to low prospecting and bad pipeline development activity. If there is no sales pipeline the organisation may go into a permanent decline. Organisations/salespeople who are not proactive developing their sales pipeline can end up not hitting their sales forecasts as new business is essential to their success (Sohnchen and Albers, 2010). This is in stark contrast to the salespeople/organisations who have a very pro-active approach to the sales pipeline and a continuing revenue stream. It is important that sales managers agree with the salespeople (and the organisation) on the definition of what a qualified prospect is. An example could be that a qualified prospect may be one that can sign an order within 90 days, whereas in another organisation it may be 30 days or even 7 days. Having the pipeline of qualified prospects can indicate consistent sales activity by the salesperson. A steady stream of worthy leads is practically nirvana for the organisation (Trailer and Dickie, 2006). It is also worth remembering that social media is essential to the front end (customer acquisition) of the B2B sales process, but every step in the sales process should now have a social media role element (Schuldt and Totten, 2015). Salespeople can dramatically speed up the prospecting process by using the correct social media platform to find qualified prospects and to also help ideal prospects find the organisation (developed further in Chapter 3).

The sales cycle is important as it identifies exactly where there are revenue opportunities, and this can help determine if forecasts are going to be on target or if corrective action needs to be taken. It is also important to review all deals to determine if any of them are dead. If this activity does not take place, then they may end up with an over-inflated pipeline which looks good on paper but nowhere resembles reality. All opportunities have a shelf life and meeting with the sales team on a regular basis helps to cleanse the pipeline. Pipeline management needs to focus on value, velocity and win rate, which are seen as the essential pipeline success formula (Apollo, 2014). These prospects need to be qualified quickly or removed from the pipeline, since it is important to have a sales pipeline that is accurate. The automated sales pipeline can help track, individual prospects, their name, size of order, where they are in the sales cycle and the date it is likely to close. An automated sales pipeline should ideally be achieved through a CRM system. This is a customer database that collates all information on prospective and existing customers and almost all organisations now have CRM professional systems to record and analyse data (Khodakarami and Chan, 2014). CRM systems can also help with the evaluation of potential customers in the sales pipeline and give estimates of the percentage probability of closing the sale. Sales cycle velocity looks at the amount of time it takes for an opportunity to move from start to finish and from stage to stage as this can be used to help forecast the probability of closing the prospect. In terms of win rate, measuring whether the deal was won, whether a competitor won it, whether the prospect implements an internal solution, or the prospect takes no action needs to be highlighted. This type of intelligence is critical in the development of the sales team in achieving future sales.

Sales managers in the past were inclined to measure their salespeople on a qualitative basis, but our research showed that they need to look to develop more quantitative measures when reviewing how the salespeople are performing (Harmon et al., 2002). The results from our research identified measurements that can be used for the front end of the sales process. Management can implement these measurements to review progress on the prospecting activities taking place and how they are performing against any key performance indicators (KPIs) that have been set. Sales is all about numbers and it is critical management monitors the salespeople's activity levels on initial contact with prospects, appointments, and conversion. Table 1.1 sets out the measurements that can be used by organisations that can help navigate them through this prospecting journey. By doubling the number of qualified calls along with getting through to the right decision maker more often and achieving more appointments, this can lead to more sales being closed which could help generate more revenue per sale (Hopkins, 1998). All of this is doable if sales management evaluates what numbers their sales team needs to process to hit their financial goals along with monitoring their performance against these goals.

Salespeople must have a strong willpower as they get rejected many times by buyers but if they are persistent, they can achieve positive results. In sales there is the expression that a salesperson must kiss a lot of frogs before they find their prince (new customer). By measuring all the above, the sales manager will be able to see what each salesperson is achieving. This will help them identify which salespeople are underperforming and they can then work with the salesperson to help identify what the issues are. The Performance Metrics needs to be filled on a regular basis so that the sales team can review what activities are taking place in prospecting and if the qualified leads are being converted into actual sales. There needs to be a pipeline process to convert opportunities into sales, this can include, qualification of the opportunity, the strategic approach to the

Table 1.1 Pipeline Measurement Metrics

Pipeline Measurement Metrics	Frequency	Reference
Number of leads generated	Weekly	(Trailer and Dickie, 2006)
Number of qualified leads generated	Weekly	(Schiffman, 2003)
Number of referral calls	Monthly	(Schmitt et al., 2011)
Number of social media leads generated	Weekly	(Agnihotri et al., 2012)
Number of cold calls made	Weekly	(Schiffman, 2003)
Number of advancements	Monthly	(Rackham, 2011)
Number of continuations	Monthly	(Rackham, 2011)
Number of rejected cold calls	Weekly	(Calvin, 2001)
Number of decision makers spoken to	Weekly	(Stevens, 2005)
Number of agreed appointments	Monthly	(Roman and Martin, 2008)
Number of demos requested	Monthly	(Calvin, 2001)
Number of agreed proposals to be sent out	Monthly	(White, 2004)
Percentage of time spent on prospecting	Weekly	(Sabnis et al., 2013)
Number of prospects requesting literature	Monthly	(Jolson, 1986)
% Closing ratio	Monthly	(Schiffman, 2003)
Revenue from new prospects	Quarterly	(Calvin, 2001)
Numbers of successful cross-sales to customers	Monthly	(Jobber, 2010)
Number of sales objections	Weekly	(Cassell and Bird, 2009)
Number of signed contracts	Quarterly	(Calvin, 2001)
Using SFA/CRM Yes/No	Weekly	(Barker et al., 2009)

Source: Sheahan, 2020.

customer, product/service presentation, design of an offer, objection handling and closure of the sale (Sohnchen and Albers, 2010).

When marketing and sales are aligned with a weighting for the leads there is a higher conversion rate in closing the sale (Jarvinen and Taiminen, 2015). Digitalising marketing campaigns can result in winning more customers and identifying more marketing-qualified leads that are ready to be handed over to the sales team. However, evidence shows that losing prospects during the hand-off period is a problem. It is in the handover stage between marketing and salespeople where the bulk of customer engagements happen, as this is where the essential in-person interactions with the potential customer are needed to move the prospect through the pipeline to the sale (Chalaka, 2020). Traditionally, when customers want to see a demonstration they can visit an event, the organisation, participate in a breakout session or webinar and have a discussion with their salesperson. Due to the Covid pandemic more and more of these activities are happening virtually through different types of sales interaction. Webinars have become one of the most powerful tools to accelerate help educate buyers, and sessions with experts are essential to convince customers to move towards a new technology or new solution. Consequently, it is recommended that marketing and sales teams engage through all media available to participate in market-qualifying meetings with customers so that these all-important interactions can happen. Where these interactions are with sales or marketing, it is where they can answer prospects' questions, respond to objections, provide education, and manage negotiations. The same goes for meetings with the decision-making units in B2B engagements or any other situation where multiple people must meet to solve buying problems and discuss sales solutions. These customer meetings are necessary so that the sales team can convert enquiries into solid sales (Chalaka, 2020).

Conclusions

In this chapter, we have highlighted some of the current issues that are affecting sales activities. We have also tried to identify some of the research that has been taking place in the last few years to shed light on these issues. Sales activities are increasingly associated with relationship management, technology and solution development. It has been noted that relationship selling is significantly more important in sectors that are people or processes based (especially where their supply chain processes need to be integrated with those of the customer), and where the goods/services are expensive, complex or where customisation is required. Salespeople must be excellent at networking, not just to build relations with customers, but also to build relationships within the organisation and with external organisations as part of their boundary-spanning role. To achieve this goal, the salesperson's main tasks consist of prospecting, implementing sales and marketing strategies, providing services, relationship management, handing complaints, self-management and database and knowledge management, which still sounds like the augmented seven steps of selling!

Perhaps the most noticeable manifestation in B2B selling is the emergence of customer relationship management that creates the need for salespeople to develop new strategies to handle different types of customers which will be explored further in Chapter 2. With the growth of online order processing and replenishment, many transactions are now effectively being managed by the marketing and/or IT functions. Consequently, order-taking, which is traditionally a sales preserve, has effectively become more of partnerships with other functions within the organisation that will be explored further in Chapter 3. Sales Management continues to evolve, and the expansion of CRM systems is providing them with far more information about their customers behaviours and the performance of salespeople. This informational development is a double-edged sword as sales managers now need to interact with different actors in the supply chain and expand their networking skills, which will be explored further in Chapter 4. B2B buyers have a great deal more information readily available and they are more sophisticated and the role of sales automation technology and social media in sales processes will be explored further in Chapter five.

References

Agnihotri, R., Kothandaraman, P., Kashyap, R., and Singh, R. (2012). Bringing "social" into sales; the impact of salespeople's social media use on service behaviours and value creation. *Journal of Personal Selling and Sales Management*, 32(3), 333–348.

Agnihotri, R., Trainor, K. J., Itani, O. S., and Rodriguez, M. (2017). Examining the role of sales-based CRM technology and social media use on post-sale service behaviors in India. *Journal of Business Research*, 81, 144–154.

Apollo, B. (2014). *12 Considerations that should be on every Chasm Crosser's Checklist*. Retrieved from https://www.inflexion-point.com/Blog/bid/70928/12-Considerations-That-Should-be-on-Every-Chasm-Crosser-s-Checklist. (Accessed: November 12, 2022).

Arli, D., Bauer, C., and Palmatier, R. W. (2018). Relational selling: Past, present and future. *Industrial Marketing Management*, 69, 169–184.

Barker, D. S., and Delpechitre, D. (2013). Collectivistic and individualistic performance expectancy in the utilization of sales automation technology in an international field sales setting. *Journal of Personal Selling and Sales Management*, 33(3), 277–288.

Baker, R., Gohmann, S., Guan, J., and Faulds, D. (2009). Why is my sales force automation system failing. *Industrial Marketing Management*, 52, 233–241.

Bean, J. (2022). 4 principles of the Consultative Sales Approach, Zendesk UK. Available at: https://www.zendesk.co.uk/blog/4-principles-of-the-consultative-sales-approach/. (Accessed: November 12, 2022).

Borg, W. S., and Young, L. (2014). Continuing the evolution of the selling process: A multi-level perspective. *Industrial Marketing Management*, 43 (4), 543–552.

Calvin, R. J. (2001). *Sales Management*. New York: Mc Graw Hill.

Cassell, J., and Bird, T. (2009). *Brilliant Selling*. London: Pearson Education.

Castro-González, S., and Bande, B. (2019). The changing role of the salesperson: How should salespeople act today? *Development and Learning in Organisations*, 33 (6), 8–11.

Chalaka, R. (2020). MQLs are Passee – are you generating MQMs? Available at: https://martech.zone/mql-vs-mqm-virtual-meetings/. (Accessed: November 12, 2022).

Corsaro, D., and D'Amico, V. (2022). How the digital transformation from COVID-19 affected the relational approaches in B2B. *Journal of Business and Industrial Marketing*, 37 (10), 2095–2115.

Cuevas, J. M. (2018). The transformation of professional selling: Implications for leading the modern sales organization. *Industrial Marketing Management*, 69, 198–208.

Drucker, P. F. (1986). *"The Frontiers of Management"*. Oxford: Butterworth-Heinemann.

Dubinsky, A. J. (1981). A factor analytic study of the personal selling process. *Journal of Personal Selling & Sales Management*, 1 (1), 26–33.

Flaherty, K., Lam, S. K., Lee, N., Mulki, J. P., and Dixon, A. L. (2012). Social network theory and the sales manager role: Engineering the right relationship flows. *Journal of Personal Selling and Sales Management*, 32 (1), 29–40.

Grewar, R., Lilien, G. L., Bhjaradwaj, S., Jindal, P., Kayande, U., Lusch, R. F., Mantrala, M., Palmatier, R. W., Rindfleisch, A., Scheer, L. K., Spekman, R., and Sridhar, S. (2015). Business-to-Business buying: Challenges and opportunities. *Customer Needs and Solutions*, 2 (3), 193–208.

Guenzi, P., and Habel, J. (2020). Mastering the digital transformation of sales. *California Management Review*, 62 (4), 57–85.

Guenzi, P., Sajtos, L., and Troilo, G. (2016). The dual mechanism of sales capabilities in influencing organizational performance. *Journal of Business Research*, 69 (9), 3707–3713.

Harmon, H. A., Hammond, K. L., Widing, R. E., and Brown, G. (2002). Exploring the sales manager's feedback to a failed sales effort. *Journal of Business and Industrial Marketing*, 17 (1), 43–55.

Hartmann, N. N., and Lussier, B. (2020), Managing the sales force through the unexpected exogenous COVID-19 crisis. Industrial Marketing Management 88: 101–111.

Hartmann, N., Plouffe, C. R., Kohsuwan, P. and Cote, J. A. (2020). Salesperson influence tactics and the buying agent purchase decision: Mediating role of buying agent trust of the salesperson and moderating role of buying agent regulatory orientation focus. *Industrial Marketing Management*, 87, 31–46.

Henshall, A. (2019). *The Most Effective Sales Negotiation Skills to Boost Customer Satisfaction*. Available from: https://www.process.st/negotiation-skills/. (Accessed: November 3, 2022).

Hopkins, T. (1998). *Sales Prospecting for Dummies* (Vol. 1). New Jersey: Wiley Publishing Inc.

Hughes, D. E., Le Bon, J., and Rapp, A. (2013). Gaining and leveraging customer-based competitive intelligence: The pivotal role of social capital and salesperson adaptive selling skills. *Journal of the Academy of Marketing Science*, 41 (1), 91–110.

Jaakkola, M., Frosen, J., and Tikkaned, H. (2015). Various forms of value-based selling capability-Commentary on Value-Based Selling: An organisational capability perspective. *Industrial Marketing Management*, 45 (1), 1–7.

Jarvinen, J., and Taiminen, H. (2015). Harnessing marketing automation for B2B content marketing. *Industrial Marketing Management*, 54, 164–175.

Jobber, D. (2010). *Principles and Practice of Marketing* (Sixth ed.). Maidenhead: McGraw-Hill.

Jolson, J. W. (1996). Qualifying sales leads the tight and loose approaches. *Industrial Marketing Management*, 17 (3), 189–196.

Jolson, M. A. (1986). Prospecting by Telephone Prenotification: An Application of the Foot-In-The-Door Technique. *Journal of Personal Selling & Sales Management*, 6 (2), 39–42.

Kaski, T. A., Hautamaki, P., Pullins, E. B., and Kock, H. (2017). Buyer versus salesperson expectations for an initial B2B sales meeting. *Journal of Business and Industrial Marketing*, 32(1), 46–56.

Khodakarami, F., and Chan, Y. E. (2014). Exploring the role of customer relationship management (CRM) systems in customer knowledge creation. *Information and Management*, 51 (1), 27–42.

Knight, R. (22 May 2017). How to improve your sales skills, even if you're not a salesperson. *Harvard Business Review*. Available from: https://hbr.org/2017/05/how-to-improve-your-sales-skills-even-if-youre-not-a-salesperson. (Accessed: November 1, 2022).

Krogue, K. (2018). Why sales reps spend less than 36% of time selling (and less than 18% in CRM), Forbes. Forbes Magazine. Available at: https://www.forbes.com/sites/kenkrogue/2018/01/10/why-sales-reps-spend-less-than-36-of-time-selling-and-less-than-18-in-crm/?sh=48eae8aab998. (Accessed: November 3, 2022).

Marshall, G. W., Moncrief, W. C., Rudd, J. M., and Lee, N. (2012). Revolution in sales: The impact of social media and related technology on the selling environment. *Journal of Personal Selling and Sales Management*, 32 (3), 349–363.

Moncrief, W. C., and Marshall, G. W. (2005). The evolution of the seven steps of selling. *Industrial Marketing Management*, 34 (1), 13–22.

Moncrief, W. C. (2017). Are sales as we know it dying ... or merely transforming. *Journal of Personal Selling and Sales Management*, 37 (4), 271–279.

Moore, N. J., Raymond, A., and Hopkins, D. C. (2015). Social selling: A comparison of social media usage across process stage, markets and sales job functions. *Journal of Marketing Theory and Practice*, 23 (1), 1–20.

Negley, H. (2022). *The Salesforce Consultant's Guide: Tools to Implement or Improve Your Client's Salesforce Solution.* New York. Springer publishing.

Peters, L., Ivens, B. S., and Pardo, C. (2020). Identification as a challenge in key account management: Conceptual foundations and a qualitative study. *Industrial marketing Management*, 90 (7), 200–213.

Rackham, N. (2011). *Spin Selling.* Aldershot: Gower Publishing Limited.

Rangarajan, D., Sharma, A., Lyngdoh, T., and Paesbrugghe, B. (2021). Business-to-business selling in the post-COVID-19 era: Developing an adaptive sales force. Business Horizons, 64 (5), 647–658.

Rapp, A., and Beeler, L. (2021). The state of selling & sales management research: A review and future research agenda. *Journal of marketing Theory and Practice*, 29 (1), 37–40.

Rapp, A., and Panagopoulos, N. G. (2012). Perspectives on personal selling and social media: Introduction to the special issue. *Journal of Personal Selling and Sales Management*, 32 (3), 301–304.

Roman, S., and Martin, J. P. (2008). Changes in sales call frequency, A longitudinal examination of the consequences in the supplier-customer relationship. *Industrial Marketing Management*, 37, 554–564.

Ryan, G., Harrison, E., Plotkin, C. L., Spillecke, D., and Stanley, J. (2020). The B2B digital inflection point: How B2B sales have changed during COVID. *McKinsey and Company*, Available at: https://www.mckinsey.com/capabilities/growthmarketing-and-sales/our-insights/these-eight-charts-show-how-covid-19-has-changed-b2bsales-forever. (Accessed: December 12, 2022).

Sabnis, G., Chatterjee, C. S., Grewal, R., and Lilien, L. G. (2013). The sales lead black hole: On sales reps follow-up of marketing leads. *Journal of Marketing*, 77 (1), 52–67.

Salomonson, N., Aberg, A., and Allwood, J. (2012). Communication skills that support value creation. *Industrial Marketing Management*, 41 (1), 145–155.

Schiffman, S. (2003). *Cold Calling Techniques* (5th ed.). Avon, MA: Adams Media.

Schmitt, P., Skiera, B., and Bulte, V. D. C. (2011). Referral programs and customer value. *Journal of Marketing*, 75 (1), 46–59.

Schuldt, A. B., and Totten, W. J. (2015). Application of social media types in the sales process. *Academy of Marketing Studies Journal*, 19 (3), R230.

Sheahan, Kieran (2020). Developing and Empirically Testing a Sales Pipeline Execution Process Framework. PhD Thesis. Technological University, Dublin.

Sleep, S., Dixon, A. L., DeCarlo, T., and Lam, S. K. (2020). The business-to-business inside sales force: roles, configurations and research agenda. *European Journal of Marketing*, 54 (5), 1025–1060.

Sohnchen, F., and Albers, S. (2010). Pipeline Management for the acquisition of industrial projects. *Industrial Marketing Management*, 39 (8), 1356–1364.

Stevens, M. (2005). *Your Marketing Sucks*. New York: Crown Publishing Group.

Storbacka, K., Ryals, L., Davies, I. A., and Nenonen, S. (2009). The changing role of sales: viewing sales as a strategic, cross-functional process. *European Journal of Marketing*, 43 (7/8), 890–906.

Syam, N., and Sharma, A. (2018). Waiting for a sales renaissance in the fourth industrial revolution: Machine learning and artificial intelligence in sales research and practice. *Industrial Marketing Management*, 69, 135–146.

The Rain Group: Getting buyers to (2020). Available at: https://www.rainsalestraining.com/blog/9-ways-to-influence-buyer-purchase-decisions. (Accessed: July 3, 2022).

Trailer, B., and Dickie, J. (2006). Understanding what your sales manager is up against. *Harvard Business Review*, 84 (7–8), 48–55.

Wagner, A. J., and Mai, E. (2015). What are they thinking? Establishing seller credibility through sales presentation strategy. *International Journal of Sales, Retailing and Marketing*, 4 (6), 3–17.

Webb, K. L., and Hogan, J. E. (2002). Hybrid channel conflict: causes and effects on channel performance. *The Journal of Business & Industrial Marketing*, 17 (5), 338–356.

White, M. (2004). *The First 90 days and Beyond: An Operating Guide for New Sales Managers*. Indiana: Author House.

Yu, P. Y., and Cai, Q. S. (2007). A new approach to customer targeting under conditions of information shortage. *Marketing Intelligence and Planning*, 25 (4), 343–359.

2 Relationship Selling and Value in Sales Interactions

Introduction

In this chapter, we consider the relationship between buyers and sellers, and what buyers require from their interactions with the selling organisation. This issue needs to be addressed as many selling organisations have decided how they wish to interact with the customer as it allows them to manage the relationship in a way that provides value to them. This can lead to an homogenous offer across the market, which may overservice some customers and underserve others. One of the key skills of the salesperson is listening to what the customer wants, or they could waste time and resources trying to develop the relationship in the wrong way. Buyers have identified that many salespeople have poor listening skills, and they fail to adjust their dialogue accordingly (Kaski, Niemi and Pullins, 2018). Salespeople need to ensure that they can identify the type of relationship/interaction that the customer needs as this allows them to align their messages and activities to the customers' requirements, so that they can fulfil or exceed the customers' expectations. Therefore, it is critical to understand the value required by customers in their interactions with the selling organisation, and to always remember that it is what the customer appreciates that is important and not what is being sold to them (Cuevas, 2018).

Most B2B buying organisations purchase from a network of suppliers to procure the range of products and services to support their operation. However, these buyers do not always require the same type of sales relationship with each selling organisation. Sales managers can help salespeople to gain the maximum utility from their B2B relationships by emphasising the sales attributes or features that align with the buying organisations' preferences and that will provide the greatest value for both parties. We consider the growing importance of aligning the sales organisation's objectives with buyer value perceptions to generate value co-creation (e.g., Aitken and Paton, 2016; Baumann, Le Meunier-FitzHugh and Wilson, 2017). There is considerable literature on key account management

DOI: 10.4324/9781003173892-2

(Davies and Ryals, 2014; Peters, Ivens and Pardo, 2020; Sonkova and Grabowska, 2015) and relationship marketing commitment (Morgan and Hunt, 1994) that provides further insights to help identify what buying organisations value in their relationships with their suppliers.

Relationship Selling

Relationship selling has been at the forefront of marketing practice and research for several years, driven by rapid developments in technologies and changing customer needs (e.g., Palmatier et al., 2013). Relationship selling has been recognised as a key component of business growth. Researchers have evaluated different types of relationships within the buying and selling and around the sales process to consider how these can be used to increase sales (Borg and Young, 2014). Sales Managers' efforts are focussed at adapting a sales organisation so that it is ready for change. Buyers see the importance of supplier relationship orientation and know that this is critical to the success of their own company's performance. Supplier relationship orientation also helps suppliers to view this customer engagement as a positive step which in turn helps to keep them motivated in investing their time to help the customer. Recently research has focussed upon the early stages of the sales process, which provides organisations with opportunities for early relationship building by integrating the changes in the evolution of the sales process into a framework (Kaski, Niemi and Pullins, 2018).

Do buyers buy people or buy conversations? This is a key question that is being explored considering the new post-Covid sales landscape. In the past, salespeople met with the buyers face-to-face but during the pandemic this all changed due to travel and quarantine restrictions. Salespeople recognise the value of relationship selling and the need to build strong virtual relationships along with having good conversations with the buyers. Salespeople need to contact the people in a customer's buying centre where they need to establish a good rapport with industry experts, lead customers and decision makers as all these people may have an influence on the buyer making a positive decision in buying the suppliers product or service (Kaski, Niemi and Pullins, 2018). The effectiveness of the salesperson in building a relationship during the interaction with the prospect is critical to the sales success (Varghese and Edward, 2015). Selling has also been called a creative process that does not rely on selling principles/practice alone. The consummate salesperson offers leadership and can effectively respond to unexpected events through the timely, practical application of marketplace knowledge and modern selling techniques (Chonko, 2022). This ability elevates customer relationship building to an art-form.

Borg and Young (2014, p.550) considered relational selling and presented a multi-level selling process model with the focus on interpersonal relationship elements and they highlighted that "the phenomena that we seek to understand – the flow of activities which constitutes the sales process – will undoubtedly continue to evolve". Researchers are evaluating the number of relationships within the buying and selling area of the sales process, and how these can be maximised to increase sales (Borg and Young, 2014). While relationship selling is seen to be important, since it is at the back end of the sales process in acquiring new customers, it has been identified that it is also critical to build relationships with the prospects at the early part or the front end of the sales process (Sheahan, 2020). The results of this research brought a new dimension to relationship building through the acquisition process. It was felt that it was a perfect opportunity to demonstrate to the prospective customer that they knew what they were doing by responding quickly to customer enquiries and that they could deliver on their commitments. Arli, Bauer and Palmatier (2018) carried out an in-depth review of relationship selling where they emphasised that companies need to seek ways to add value, be more efficient in communication and make sure responses to buyers are timely. They highlighted that much remains to be learned about the effectiveness of relationship-selling strategies for customer acquisition.

Research has highlighted that building trust with the prospective customer was also critical to ongoing relationships as without this trust the buyer/seller relationship or partnership would not exist (Kaski, Niemi and Pullins, 2017; Magus et al., 2023). Arli, Bauer and Palmatier (2018) discuss trust and commitment as emerging conditions in understanding how to build customer relationships effectively. Salespeople are frequently considered as trusted advisers in that they are believed to be competent, have integrity and a rapport that allows them to maintain a positive customer focus and keep their promises (Chonko, 2022). Trust may be viewed from two perspectives, active (based on performance) and passive (absence of worry). The significance of this is that beliefs and opinions may become uncertainty or misconception of reality that can be countered through communications from a trusted salesperson. Buyers see trust as a foundation stone to trusting relationships because highly confidential information is going to be shared and the buyers need to feel comfortable that their data is in safe hands (Brockman, Parkb and Morganc, 2017). Conveying a strong unifying message through communications that are underpinned by truthfulness and transparency can help to build trust.

Salespeople should focus their efforts on building strong relationships with higher-performing customers and prospects that can offer longer lifetime value and profits (Rapp et al., 2014), but they should frequently review their communications within these relationships to ensure that they are still perceived as trustworthy. However, it has also been highlighted recently that salespeople can overestimate their customers trust in their communications. This overestimation of trust within the B2B relationship has been found to have severe consequences such as negative Word of Mouth (WOM), as well as potentially costing the organisation millions in lost revenue, indicating that there can be limits to the benefits of long-term sales relationships especially when there are unrealistic expectations and/or misunderstood intention (Magus et al., 2023). Integrity also came across as important especially when making commitments to the customers. These traits are particularly valuable to larger customers in long-term relationships (Le Meunier-FitzHugh Cometto and Johnson, 2021). Long-term relationship selling has been discussed extensively in the literature and when it comes to key account management, it is often linked to selling to customers who are important to the supplier (Peters, Ivens and Pardo, 2020).

Key Account Management (KAM)

Dedicated key accounts are a lot more common as sales organisations are recognising the value in fostering close relationships with key strategic customers (Bradford et al., 2012). Woodburn and McDonald (2012:2) define KAM as "a supplier led process of inter-organisational collaboration that creates unique value for both supplier and strategically important customers". Key account relationships are also described as "the systematic supplier process for managing strategically important business-to-business relationships" (Davies and Ryals, 2014:3). KAM interactions takes place internally within the organisation and externally with the customer's organisation. Internally, the key account manager needs to work with the various departments to create the value proposition and to understand what is being offered to their customer. A study highlighted that where there is a higher level of internal collaboration there is a higher level of performance of the key account manager (Murphy and Coughlan, 2018). The same result applies to external interactions and interestingly when both interactions were collaborative, there was an even stronger joint effect on performance. KAM relationships can be carried out by a dedicated team or a fluid team. Fluid teams are normally set up for a specific customer opportunity and disband once the opportunity is closed out (Lai and Yang, 2017). The selection of key accounts are decided not only by the size or monetary purchases of the customers but also on how strategic these accounts are to the supplier organisation (Fazli-Salehi, Torres and Zúñiga, 2021).

Key to the success of KAM is understanding the importance of relationship quality and social capital to value creation (Badawi, Battor and Badghish, 2021). Retaining these key accounts is extremely challenging and customer defection rates are a concern (Schreier and Prugl, 2008). However, the reason why key customers change suppliers is not always understood. It is reported that some customers see suppliers becoming complacent and lackadaisical within the relationship, and this can act as a catalyst to terminate the relationship, even a long-term KAM relationship (Friend and Johnson, 2017). The key account sales team that accurately targets those of its customers who are likely to make profitable purchases that will make a much better return on its marketing investment than its competitors who do not engage in this activity (Kumar, Petersen and Leone, 2007). The importance of collaborative interactions in a B2B context suggests that a relationship is being built between organisations and their customers that should help to build loyalty between them. One of the drawbacks is that the stronger a customer's loyalty the greater the amount of discount the buyer looks for from the supplier (Wieseke, Alavi and Habel, 2014). Additionally, the customer can think that they are so embedded in the supplier's relationship that they can ask for anything that suits their business requirements and therefore suppliers need to be aware of the dangers in getting too close to the customer.

The most effective senior managers play a key role in facilitating key account management-buyer-seller relationships to help improve gains for their business (Pereira et al., 2019). Suppliers can invest a lot of their time in key account management and it is important they try and achieve a good return in their investment. The covid pandemic brought serious challenges to sales teams in trying to develop collaborative interactions with customers as negotiations could no longer be carried out face-to-face and suppliers had to transform themselves by moving to a virtual environment to deal with these challenges (Ewe and Ho, 2022). In a post-pandemic world, KAM participants have made a significant move from face-to-face meetings to a more flexible working approaches, using the available new virtual tools (Lacoste, Zidani and Cuevas, 2022). It is recognised that sales organisations will need to adapt to these new hybrid systems. To support these changes KAMs will need to improve the quality of their presentations and their sales pitches online to build key account relationships with their customers (Rangarajan et al., 2021).

Value Creation in B2B Sales Relationships

The role of B2B sales in creating value is widely recognised (e.g., Haas, Snehota and Corsaro, 2012). While the concept that understanding and leveraging customer value has been a topic for debate for some time (e.g., Macdonald et al., 2011), there are some aspects of value creation that are still being developed. One of these aspects is reciprocal value propositions (Lindgreen et al., 2012). It is generally accepted that value is created through a trade-off between perceived benefits and the accompanying cost of acquiring a particular good or service. The basis of this theory is exchange theory of value from economics (Haas, Snehota and Corsaro, 2012). However, this view has evolved, and value of exchange has become embedded in the interaction of buyers and sellers to negotiate a valued solution. Creating value within B2B relationships has recently undergone a series of rapid changes (Almquist, Cleghorn and Sherer, 2018; Rustholkarhu, Hautamaki and Aaikka-Stenroos, 2021). Customers are increasingly seen as active partners rather than a passive target for the organisation's value proposition. It is suggested that this joint value realisation engenders episode value in one-off transactions, as well as extended relationship value in continuing exchanges (Baumann and Le Meunier-FitzHugh, 2014).

The key concern is that there is not one clear description of 'value', as the concept is perceptual. Corsaro (2014, p. 992) points out that "the way in which the customer approaches and sees value can differ from the way the company does." From the company's point of view value creation has three steps: *choose the value* (i.e., positioning the offer), *provide the value* (i.e., developing, producing and distributing products and services) and finally *communicate the value* through marketing activities and the sales force (Kowalkowski et al., 2012). However, this may not be the value that the customer is realising or even seeking as value is now also located in the customers' interactions with the sellers as well as in the product. As the group that has the closest interaction with the customer, salespeople are most able to gauge customers value perceptions, both expressed and latent, and to understand what is the value that is sought (Haas, Snehota and Corsaro, 2012; Terho et al., 2012). Salespeople are also well placed to cultivate social, empathic and emotional ties with customers while providing relationship value elements such as expertise, clear communications (transparency) and trust (integrity). In a recent study, Almquist, Cleghorn and Sherer (2018) identifed 40 'elements of value' that could be generated through buyer/serller interactions. These 40 elements were refined down to five categories – inspiration value, individual value, ease of doing business, functional value and table stakes.

For example, organisations are using Value Based Selling (VBS) as part of their sales strategy. VBS is where the salesperson aims to provide value to the customer at every stage of the selling process and they will therefore need clear guidance and training from the sales leader for it to be successful. Toytari and Rajala (2015) identified a VBS approach using planning, implementation, and information leverage to maximise the opportunities for the marketers and sales in getting the messages across to their customers. However, it is critical that sales management supports this effort and sales teams are included in communications and planning, as without this support VBS across the organisation would not be successful. Sales management needs to have a good understanding on what motivates their sales teams and what actions they need to take

(Miao and Evans, 2014). Baumann, Le Meunier-FitzHugh and Wilson (2017) found that in a service context, customers actively engage in value co-creation by adding their own resources to the interaction with the salesperson. Additionally, customers did not just appreciate the relationship value elements mentioned above, they also placed value on the genuine relationship with the salesperson, relying on their advice and using them to interact with other participants in the network. This finding highlighted the intricacies of creating value propositions as there is a divergence of what is considered to be valuable between the customer and salesperson (Baumann, Le Meunier-FitzHugh and Wilson, 2017).

Value can be created intentionally or unintentionally through various interactions (on or off-line) and salespeople should be aware that while they may have clarity on the value that they are trying to convey (Rustholkarhu, Hautamaki and Aaikka-Stenroos, 2021). However, the value that is being intentionally created may not always be aligned with the customers' value perception. Further, customers bring their own value proposition to the interaction and the salesperson may have to adapt their sales interactions to take this into account. Rustholkarhu, Hautamaki and Aaikka-Stenroos (2021) explored how the concept of value-creation is being altered through the growth of digitally conveyed interactions. B2B customers engaging with digital interactions are less likely to identify with a salesperson, but rather may transfer their relationship to the organisation's brand personality. Under these circumstances it was found that value was co-created through dialogic interactions within digital ecosystems. However, the generated value may be difficult to measure as it is influenced by a range of unidirectional interactions that inform trust, such as blogs and posts, within the ecosystem (Hartmann, Wieland and Vargo, 2018). The fact remains that relationship value can be created through traditional interactions or digitally, and that trust remains a central concept to the buyer-seller relationships.

Sellers' Relationships with Buyers

Relationship marketing continues to advocate the importance of sellers and salespeople building long-term value in their interactions with customers (e.g., Zhang et al., 2016). The key foundation to building relationships is said to be establishing engagement and rapport, which involves finding a mutual connection and understanding of each other's needs (Kaski, Niemi and Pullins, 2018). The ability to sell with a high level of customisation and engagement, and with solution co-creations will require a degree of commitment, rapport and intimacy from both parties (Rapp et al., 2017; Sharma and Iyer, 2011). There are also various studies concerning the importance of sellers adapting their interactions to the buyer's needs resulting in co-created value (e.g., Haas,

Snehota and Corsaro, 2012; Viio and Gronroos, 2016). However, not all customers want the same sales experience in their interactions with sellers, nor do they require the same type of relationship (e.g., Hibbard et al., 2003; Palmatier et al., 2013; Spekman and Carraway, 2006). Engaging with customers at the right level by providing the correct level of interaction and frequency contributes to the realisation of the relationship potential.

Although 'value' as a term appears frequently in sales and marketing literature it has several conceptual connotations (e.g., 'added value' or 'high-value customers'), and it is still deemed to an elusive concept by many selling organisations (e.g., Grönroos and Voima, 2013). Value has been defined as an "interactive relativistic preference experience" (Holbrook, 2006, p. 212), which can be embedded in the relationship between a buyer and a sales offering (service or product) (Baumann, Le Meunier-FitzHugh and Wilson, 2017). The success of the sales interaction is dependent on the adaptation of the offer as influenced by the buyer-seller relationship orientation (Viio and Gronroos, 2016). It has also been suggested that a study of actor engagement would help to make value co-creation elements observable and therefore manageable (Storbacka et al., 2016). Sales relationships need to be adapted to the buyer's requirements and are influenced not only by what buyers' prefer but also the value of the product (good or service) being traded. *Value* is therefore selected as the first element of the types of sales relationships (see Figure 2.1). The outcome of an extended, committed relationship

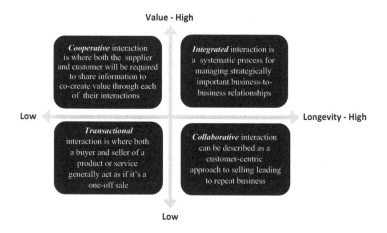

Figure 2.1 Types of Sales Relationships.
Source: Le Meunier-FitzHugh and FitzHugh, (2018).

can be the ability to co-create value, and this relationship can change over time (Lusch, Vargo and Gustafsson, 2016). Committed relationships consist of intertwined exchange episodes developed over time and it is therefore reasonable to include *Longevity* as the second variable of the type of sales relationship (see Figure 2.1). Consequently, identifying the attributes that facilitate the buyer/seller relationship should help sellers to provide the most appropriate interaction in each selling situation to generate value for both parties.

The extant literature indicates that there are several relationship concepts that relate to positive buyer/seller relationships, such as clear communications, reputation, ease of doing business and trust (e.g., Palmatier et al., 2013). Rapport relates to the concept of trust, as it helps to build credibility and interpersonal connections (Kaski, Niemi and Pullins, 2018; Manning, Ahearne and Reece, 2012). Intimacy is an indicator of strong relationship ties with customers built on customer insights and understanding. Rapport and trust also relate to levels of intimacy that is needed to support the required inter-company learning, especially in complex sales relationships where the activities of the partnering companies need to be aligned to be successful (Brock and Zhou, 2012; Kaski, Niemi and Pullins, 2018).

The assumption is that extended interactions generate value for the participants through trust and learning-based cooperation (Sales-Vivo, Gil-Saura and Gallarza, 2020). However, some studies have adopted a broader view of long-term relationships that indicate that there may be a misalignment in the required value in interaction (Baumann, Le Meunier-FitzHugh and Wilson, 2017) or even relationship performance degradation (Hibbard et al., 2003).

Relationship longevity may bias the company's future evaluation and expectation of benefits of the relationship as knowledge redundancy and relationship inertia become established (e.g., Nordhoff et al., 2011; Zhang et al., 2021). Therefore, it is also reasonable to assume that not all sales exchanges should be based on committed, long-term exchanges, but that some will still need a degree of intimacy and rapport to make them work. It is also worth noting that some buyers are only interested in a transactional interaction with the seller even if they have been trading with them for a long-time. This may be due to the culture of the buying organisation and/or the good or services that are being sold. Therefore, some sales interactions will be driven by the need of the buyer to negotiate every individual transaction with the seller to gain the most advantageous terms. Culture also plays a part in value creation within the sales organisation. A strong sales culture can provide some very advantageous outcomes when it is developed properly it can assist in providing an important source in achieving competitive advantage (Barnes et al., 2006).

Four types of sales interactions have been identified by Le Meunier-FitzHugh and FitzHugh (2018) (See Figure 2.1). The classifications are based on the required levels of value and longevity of the various buyer/seller interactions, rather than a relationship evolution. The four types of interactions are labelled Transactional, Cooperative, Collaborative and Integrated. These four interaction types cover most sales interactions. Unless the selling organisation completely understands the type of interaction that the buyer requires and can emphasise the appropriate sales attributes during their interactions, they will not be able to create the greatest value or be at their most productive (Aitken and Paton, 2016; Haas, Snehota and Corsaro, 2012). In the busy, high-pressure business-to-business (B2B) sales arena it is important for the organisation to understand how to engage with their customers, as the cost of acquiring and managing customers has increased over time.

It is essential for the selling organisation to be operating at the right level for each interaction as each organisation purchases from a network of suppliers. A Transactional or 'arms-length' relationships is where both the buyer(s) and seller(s) of a product generally act independently from one other, with little incentive to form an on-going relationship (Brock and Zhou, 2012). Transactional relationships were generally generated lower returns for the seller and were often characterized by price rigidity, which may explain the selling organisation's desire to extend into longer-term relationships. In a Transactional relationship it was found that only four attributes were highlighted in their relationships with their suppliers, which were *price, performance, ease of doing business* and *contractual obligations.* The ability to negotiate a keen price was found to be the main attribute, supported by product performance and ease of doing business while meeting contractual obligations were an indication of efficient processes. One of the key messages that came from buyers was that not all suppliers were able to accept this reality and wasted a lot of effort focusing on relational attributes that the buyer did not consider relevant especially for lower-value products. This was compounded by some organisations' culture was to maintain transactional sales relationships with their commodity suppliers to get the best price on every transaction.

Cooperative relationships usually involve selling products that have a higher value to the buying organisation. These are frequently single exchanges for high-cost, high-value products such as production equipment, consultancy services and construction projects, where a more intimate relationship is required so that information exchanges from both the supplier and customer are needed to enable the generation of value through their interactions (Baumann, Le Meunier-FitzHugh and Wilson, 2017; Viio and Gronroos, 2014). With this change in relationship, the number of selling attributes that were important in the interaction increased to six, *communication, performance, price, trust, co-creation,* and *reputation* (Le Meunier-FitzHugh and FitzHugh, 2018). Clear communications that include areas such as current offers and product availability was at the top of the list, followed by product performance and competitive pricing. As these sales interactions require greater intimacy to generate value, the emphasis moves then from tangible to more intangible attributes. In a Cooperative relationship, the buyer needs to trust that the selling organisation is acting in their best interest, so that they can exchange knowledge and co-create value within their interactions, even during their initial exchanges, or value could be damaged. These two attributes (trust and co-creation) have been established in literature as underpinning intense buyer-seller relationships (Rapp et al., 2017; Sales-Vivo, Gil-Saura and Gallarza, 2020). Establishing trust and co-creation of value will also be conveyed and supported by the selling organisation's reputation. The reputation was highlighted as being important in quickly establishing cooperative relationships, as there may not be time to build up trust gradually. Selling organisations should understand how these attributes affect the buying decisions of their customers. In this cooperative selling situation, the organisation should focus on the attributes that are valued by the buyer, rather than the seller, and it is critical that the marketing materials support the brand reputation and communicates the value proposition clearly.

Collaborative relationships are established by building commitment with a customer over time. There has been a considerable amount of research focused on establishing collaborative relationships, and it has been identified that the required investment in customisation and associated risk of sharing knowledge may influence the customer/supplier power dependence and which can undermine the value for both parties (Peters, Ivens and Pardo, 2020). Longevity means that the seller can tailor solutions through these continuing relationships, which leads to repeat business and customer loyalty (Sonkova and Grabowska, 2015; Zhang et al., 2016). In the Collaborative relationship, eight significant attributes are identified by Le Meunier-FitzHugh and FitzHugh (2018). These attributes were *trust, communication, price, X-Factor, risk and reward sharing, performance, co-creation and ease of doing business.* Trust was found to be by far the most significant attribute in Collaborative relationship, so that the organisations' activities can be aligned, and critical information shared (Brock and Zhou, 2012). Transparent communications (that support trust) and the X-factor are the next two most critical sales attributes in this type of interaction.

The X-factor appears to be something of a nebulas concept. The X-factor was found to encompass a range of concepts in buyers' minds. It was described as the ability to develop strong linkages between the two parties, others as core competences (such as engineering expertise) that could add value to the buying organisation, while others saw it as some unidentifiable benefit or kudos of doing business with that supplier. However, being able to negotiate a competitive price continues to be an important attribute. It was also identified that product performance, value co-creation and ease of doing business were all significant attributes (Baumann, Le Meunier-FitzHugh and Wilson, 2017). In Collaborative relationships, it was also found that a degree of risk sharing became an important attribute. This could cover things such as investment in product development, shared marketing activities, or the selling organisation providing support staff on site. The important point is that the buying organisation want to see that the selling organisation was prepared to invest in the relationship so that both parties can benefit. This changes the emphasis for the selling organisation from a party that just supplies goods or services into one that is committed to success of both parties which then can lead to increased sales.

Integrated relationships are described by Davies and Ryals (2014:3) as "the systematic supplier process for managing strategically important business-to-business relationships". Integrated relationships (may also be called key account relationships) are those that are built up over time and have high value to both parties and where the seller responds to the higher levels of procurement sophistication of the buyer. Consequently, these relationships require considerable investment from the selling organisation as they need to obtain access to a range of internal resources so that they can develop the relevant customer value (Peters, Ivens and Pardo, 2020). These relationships are characterised by a high level of intimacy and knowledge sharing over an extended period. In an integrated relationship the need is for a high level of value is generated for both parties, which is also developed through repeated interactions. In the Integrated relationships there were 13 distinct attributes identified: *Trust, communication, business performance, co-creation, price, ease of doing business, contractual obligations, X-factor, flexibility, reputation, risk and reward sharing, sharing information,* and *cultural fit* (Le Meunier-FitzHugh and FitzHugh, 2018).

The management of key accounts has been described as providing the development of shared information and an analysis of the customer's strategic realities, their critical needs, resources and buying processes so that the selling organisation can optimise and focus their scare resources to meeting the buyer's requirements and their long-term future (Capon, 2001). Therefore, trust remains the most important attribute in Integrated relationships as the parties become increasingly interdependent over time. Communications and business performance were also identified as key attributes in the relationship. The importance of open communications and the ability of the parties to transfer and share knowledge, has been widely discussed in key account management literature (e.g., Davies and

Ryals, 2014). The aim of the Integrated relationship is to provide multiple benefits for both the buyer and seller in terms of increased sales and profits. These relationships frequently operate through co-creation exchange networks (including digital) and the buyer has much of the knowledge/power in the relationship as the seller (Sales-Vivo, Gil-Saura and Gallarza, 2020). The ability to share knowledge and be culturally compatible are essential to aligning activities and objectives between the buying and selling organisations.

In Integrated relationships three new concepts were identified as being important to the buyer/seller relationship: cultural fit, information sharing, and flexibility. Cultural fit is where the underlying values, beliefs, and attitudes of the two parties are aligned so that their interactions and processes can operate smoothly, in harmony. This was described as the willingness of suppliers 'to go the extra mile' on behalf of the buyer and the ability to collaborate on projects and sharing best practice to create supply chain efficiencies. In a key account relationship, it has been identified that it is important that the buying organisation is able to maintain a degree of flexibility to be able to respond to changing circumstances (Davies and Ryals, 2014). It was also identified that the ability for both parties to share confidential information and knowledge effectively was a critical part in their relationships as it becomes more complex and independent. This information sharing can take many different forms including financials, new product development and the future plans of the buying organisation. However, it is important to remember that this knowledge sharing should be two-way (bi-directional) as this aids in the development of a number of other attributes including trust. Negotiating on price, which was so important in Transactional relationships, remerges as an essential attribute in the Integrated relationship. This was explained as occurring when the buying organisation moves from multiple to single supplier relationships (such as key account) as they need to ensure that they are still paying a competitive price. The attributes of ease of doing business and meeting contractual obligations were identified by buyers as necessary to underpin a long-term relationship (Le Meunier-FitzHugh and FitzHugh, 2018). Removing layers of bureaucracy is apparently significant to improving business processes as the two companies become closer and align their activities. All these attributes are supportive of the growing interdependence of the buyer and seller and reinforce the need for selling organisations to engage with multiple attributes.

To support targeted sales operations that leverage customer relationships, it is necessary that salespeople should interact in a way that is aligned with the attributes that the customer values. It was identified that customers/buyers require different types of relationship depending on the type of interaction/product they want to exchange with the supplier and that different attributes were valued within in each of the four types of buyer relationship. If the selling organisation does not understand what is valued in each type of relationship, then the salesperson's time spent in front of the customer may be wasted (Chonko, 2022). Organisations should remember that not all customers want to have an integrated or even collaborative relationship with their suppliers, and that many are very happy with a transactional type of interaction that can also depend to the type and value of the product being traded. It is important to note at this point that the amount purchased by the buying organisation does not necessarily indicate what type of relationship is required, as a high turnover can be generated by multiple, transactional type interactions. It is essential that the selling organisation ensures that they have identified clearly what are the cultural norms of the buying organisation and not try to impose homogeneous relationships with all customers.

Conclusions

In this chapter, we have described the types of interactions that exist between B2B buyers and sellers. The critical objective for the research was to ensure that sellers were able to clearly identify their customer's needs and the type of relationship that they ultimately wanted. As discussed in Chapter 1, this relies on the salesperson developing high level of skills in the areas of listening and questioning. Diagnosing the problem, although often done by salespeople, does rely on organisations accepting that buyers/customers have a range of needs and that not all buying organisations want to have extended or intimate relationships with their suppliers. Unfortunately, a lot of sales training emphasise the need to treat customers in a homogenous manner, even though this may be successful at some levels, it can become counterproductive with many customers.

In summary, buyers value sales relationships that are aligned with their needs, so selling organisations need to employ market sensing skills to select the type of interaction that is appropriate to each selling situation. Second, salespeople will need to employ a greater number of sales attributes as their relationships become more complex and/or extended. Third, the order of importance of the attributes changes with each relationship type. Finally, salespeople would benefit from guidance and training on the selling attributes that are aligned with each relationship type. The implications for sales leaders are that they should be aware that not all sales relationships can be managed in the same way, so they need to employ broad-based selling skills that can meet the requirements of their customer portfolio. The need to achieve establish appropriate sales relationships so that lifetime value can be extended is explored. Integrated relationships are likely to require advanced selling skills and the seniority to be able to engage at the right level with these customers. Chapter 4 will consider the challenges of Sales Leadership.

References

Aitken, A., and Paton, R. A. (2016). Professional buyers and the value proposition. *European Management Journal*, 34 (3), 223–231.

Almquist, E., Cleghorn, J., and Sherer, L. (2018). The B2B elements of value. *Harvard Business Review*, 96 (3), 5–11.

Arli, D., Bauer, C., and Palmatier, R. W. (2018). Relational selling: Past, present and future. *Industrial Marketing Management*, 69, 169–184.

Badawi, N. S., Battor, M., and Badghish, S. (2021). Relational key account management: insights from the Middle Eastern context. *Journal of Business & Industrial Marketing*, 37 (2), 353–365.

Barnes, J., Jackson. J. W., Hutt, M., and Kumar, A. (2006). The role of culture strength in shaping sales force outcomes. *Journal of Personal Selling and Sale Management*, 26 (3), 255–270.

Baumann, J., and Le Meunier-FitzHugh, K. (2014). Trust as a facilitator of co-creation in customer-salesperson interaction – an imperative for the realization of episodic and relational value? *AMS Review*, 4 (1–2), 5–20.

Baumann, J., Le Meunier-FitzHugh, K., and Wilson, H. N. (2017). The challenge of communicating reciprocal value promises: Buyer-seller value proposition disparity in professional services. *Industrial Marketing Management*, 64 (3–4), 107–212.

Borg, W. S., and Young, L. (2014). Continuing the evolution of the selling process: A multi-level perspective. *Industrial Marketing Management*, 43 (4), 543–552.

Bradford, D. K., Challagalla, N. G., Hunter, K. G., and Moncrief, C. W. (2012). Strategic account management: Conceptualising, integrating and extending the domain from fluid to dedicated accounts. *Journal of Personal Selling & Sales Management*, 32 (1), 41–56.

Brock, J. K. U., and Zhou, J. Y. (2012). Customer Intimacy. *Journal of Business and Industrial Marketing*, 27 (5), 370–383.

Brockman, K. B., Parkb, E. J., and Morganc, M. R. (2017). The Role of Buyer Trust in Outsourced CRM: Its Influence on Organisational Learning and Performance. *Journal of Business-to-Business Marketing*, 24 (3), 201–219.

Capon, N. (2001). *Key Account Management and Planning*. New York: The Free Press.

Chonko, L. B. (2022) *Sustainable Competitive Advantage in Sales*. Cheltenham, UK: Edward Elgar.

Corsaro, D. (2014). The emergent role of value representation in managing business relationships. *Industrial Marketing Management*, 43 (6), 985–995.

Cuevas, J. M. (2018). The transformation of professional selling: Implications for leading the modern sales organization. *Industrial Marketing Management*, 59, 198–208.

Davies, I. A., and Ryals, L. J. (2014). The effectiveness of key account management practices. *Industrial Marketing Management*, 43 (7), 1182–1194.

Ewe, S. Y., and Ho, H. H. P. (2022). *Transformation of Personal Selling during and after COVID-19 Pandemic*. In: COVID-19 and the Evolving Business Environment in Asia (259–279). Springer Nature, Singapore.

Fazli-Salehi, R., Torres, I. M., and Zúñiga, M. Á. (2021). A sales approach to Key Account Management (KAM): Toward a unified view of KAM deployment and operationalization. *Services Marketing Quarterly*, 42 (3–4), 234–252.

Friend, B. S., and Johnson, S. J. (2017). Familiarity breeds contempt: perceived service and sales complacency in business to business relationships. *Journal of Personal Selling & Sales Management*, 37 (1), 42–60.

Grönroos, C., and Voima, P. (2013). Critical service logic: making sense of value creation and co-creation. *Journal of the Academy of Marketing Science*, 41 (2), 33–150.

Haas, A., Snehota, I., and Corsaro, D. (2012). Creating value in business relationships: The role of sales. *Industrial Marketing Management*, 41 (1), 94–105.

Hartmann, N. N., Wieland, H., and Vargo, S. L. (2018). Converging on a new theoretical foundation for selling. *Journal of Marketing*, 82 (2), 1–18.

Hibbard, J. D., Brunel, F. F., Dant, R. P., and Iacobucci, D. (2003). Does Relationship marketing Age Well? *Business Strategy Review*, 12 (4), 29–35.

Holbrook, M. B. (2006). Consumption experience, customer value, and subjective personal introspection: An illustrative photographic essay. *Journal of Business Research*, 59 (6), 714–725.

Kaski, T., Niemi, J., and Pullins, E. (2018). Rapport building in authentic B2B sales interaction. *Industrial Marketing Management*, 69, 235–252.

Kowalkowski, C., Persson Ridell, O., Röndell, J. G., and Sörhammar, D. (2012). The co-creative practice of forming a value proposition. *Journal of Marketing Management*, 28 (13-14), 1553–1570.

Kumar, V., Petersen, J. A., and Leone, P. R. (2007). How valuable is word of mouth. *Harvard Business Review*, 85 (10), 139–147.

Lacoste, S., Zidani, K., and Cuevas, J. M. (2022). Lateral collaboration and boundary-spanning from a global leadership perspective: The case of global account managers. *Journal of World Business*, 57 (3), 101288.

Lai, C. J., and Yang, Y. (2017). The role of formal information sharing in key account team effectiveness: does informal control matter and when. *Journal of Personal Selling & Sales Management*, 37 (4), 313–331.

Le Meunier-FitzHugh, K., and FitzHugh, L. C. (2018). *Value in Sales Interactions: A Study from the Buyer's Perspective: An Abstract.* In: Krey, N., Rossi, P. (eds) Boundary Blurred: A Seamless Customer Experience in Virtual and Real Spaces. AMSAC 2018. Developments in Marketing Science: Proceedings of the Academy of Marketing Science. Springer, Cham.

Le Meunier-FitzHugh, K., Cometto, T., and Johnson, J. (2021). Launching new global products into subsidiary markets: the vital role of sales and marketing collaboration. *Thunderbird International Business Review*, 63 (4), 1–16.

Lindgreen, A., Hingley, M. K., Grant, D. B., and Morgan, R. E. (2012). Value in business and industrial marketing: Past, present and future. *Industrial Marketing Management*, 41 (1), 207–214.

Lusch, R. F., Vargo, S. L., and Gustafsson, A. (2016). Fostering a trans-disciplinary perspectives of service ecosystems. *Journal of Business Research*, 69 (8), 2957–2963.

Macdonald, E. K., Wilson, H., Martinez, V., and Toossi, A. (2011). Assessing value-in-use: A conceptual framework and exploratory study. *Industrial Marketing Management*, 40 (5), 671–682.

Magus, S. M., Jones, E., Folse, J. A. G., and Sridhar, S. (2023). We are not on the same page: The effect of salesperson trust overestimation on customer satisfaction and relationship performance. *Industrial Marketing Management*, 109 (12), 58–70.

Manning, G. L., Ahearne, M., and Reece, B. L. (2012). *Selling Today: Partnering to Create Value*. Upper Saddle River: Prentice Hall/Pearson Education.

Miao, C. F., and Evans, K. R. (2014). Motivating industrial salesforce with sales control systems: An interactive perspective. *Journal of Business Research*, 67 (6), 1233–1242.

Morgan, R. M., and Hunt, S. D. (1994). The commitment-trust theory of relationship marketing. *Journal of Marketing*, 58 (3), 20–38.

Murphy, E. L., and Coughlan, P. J. (2018). Does it pay to be proactive? Testing proactiveness and the joint effect of internal and external collaboration on key account manager performance. *Journal of Personal Selling & Sales Management*, 38 (2), 205–219.

Noordhoff, C. S., Kyriakopoulos, K., Moorman, C., Pauwels, P., and Dellaert, B. G. (2011). The bright side and dark side of embedded ties in Business-to-Business innovation. *Journal of Marketing*, 75 (5), 34–52.

Palmatier, R. W., Houston, M. B., Dant, R. P., and Grewal, D. (2013). Relationship velocity: Towards a theory of relationship dynamics. *Journal of Marketing*, 77 (1), 13–30.

Pereira, G., Tzempelikos, N., Trento, L. R., Trento, C. R., Borchardt, M., and Viegas, C. V. (2019). Top managers' role in key account management. *Journal of Business & Industrial Marketing*, 34 (5), 977–993.

Peters, L., Ivens, B. S., and Pardo, C. (2020). Identification as a challenge in Key Account Management: Conceptual foundations and a qualitative study. *Industrial Marketing Management*, 90 (7), 200–213.

Rangarajan, D., Sharma, A., Lyngdoh, T., and Paesbrugghe, B. (2021). Business-to-business selling in the post-COVID-19 era: Developing an adaptive sales force. *Business Horizons*, 64 (5), 647–658.

Rapp, A., Bachrach, G. D., Panagopoulos, N., and Ogilvie, J. (2014). Salespeople as knowledge brokers: a review and critique of the challenger sales model. *Journal of Personal Selling & Sales Management*, 34 (4), 245–259.

Rapp, A. A., Bachrach, D. G., Flaherty, K. E., Hughes, D. E., Sharma, A., and Voorhees, C. M. (2017). The role of the sales-service interface and ambidexterity in the evolving organisation: A multilevel research agenda. *Journal of Service Research*, 20 (1), 59–75.

Rustholkarhu, S., Hautamaki, P., and Aaikka-Stenroos, L. (2021) Value (co-) creation in B2B sales ecosystems. *Journal of Business and Industrial Marketing*, 36 (4), 590–598.

Sales-Vivo, V., Gil-Saura, I., and Gallarza, M. (2020). Modelling value co-creation in triadic B2B industrial relationships. *Marketing Intelligence and Planning*, 38 (7), 941–955.

Schreier, M., and Reinhard, P. (2008). Extending lead-user theory: Antecedents and consequences of consumers' lead userness. *Journal of Product Innovation Management*, 25 (4): 331–346.

Sharma, A., and Iyer, G. R. (2011). Are pricing policies an impediment to the success of customer solutions? *Industrial Marketing Management*, 40 (5), 723–729.

Sheahan, K. (2020). Developing and Empirically Testing a Sales Pipeline Execution Process Framework. PhD Thesis. Technological University, Dublin.

Sonkova, T., and Grabowska, M. (2015). Customer engagement: transactional vs. relationship marketing. *Journal of International Studies*, 8 (1), 196–207.

Spekman, R. E., and Carraway, R. (2006). Making the transition to collaborative buyer-seller relationships: An emerging framework. *Industrial Marketing Management*, 35 (1), 10–19.

Storbacka, K., Brodie, R. J., Böhmann, T., Maglio, P. P., and Nenonen, S. (2016). Actor engagement as a microfoundation for value co-creation. *Journal of Business Research*, 69 (8), 3008–3017.

Terho, H., Haas, A., Eggert, A., and Ulaga, W. (2012). 'It's almost like taking the sales out of selling' towards a conceptualization of value-based selling in business markets. *Industrial Marketing Management*, 41 (1), 174–185.

Toytari, P., and Rajala, R. (2015). Value based selling: An organisational capability perspective. *Industrial Marketing Management*, 45, 113–114.

Varghese, J., and Edward, M. (2015). Perceived Organisational Influences on customer Orientation and Sales Performance-A Financial Services Industry Perspective. *Journal of Marketing*, 6 (2), 11–21.

Viio, P., and Gronroos, C. (2014). Value-based sales process adaptation in business relationships. *Industrial Marketing Management*, 43 (6), 1085–1095.

Viio, P., and Gronroos, C. (2016). How buyer-seller relationship orientation affects adaptation of sales processes to the buying process. *Industrial Marketing Management*, 52, 37–46.

Wieseke, J., Alavi, S., and Habel, J. (2014). Willing to pay more, eager to pay less. *Journal of Marketing*, 78 (6), 17–37.

Woodburn, D., and McDonald, M. (2012). *Key Account Management: The Definitive Guide*. John Wiley & Sons.

Zhang, J. Z., Watson, G. F., Palmatier, R. W., and Dant, R. P. (2016). Dynamic relationship marketing. *Journal of Marketing*, 80 (5), 53–75.

Zhang, Y., Leischnig, A., Heirati, N., and Hennenberg, S. C. (2021). Dark-side-effect contagion in business relationships. *Journal of Business Research*, 130 (3), 260–270.

3 Interactions Between Sales and Marketing and The Customer Journey

Introduction

Contemporary research into the interaction between sales and marketing functions forms the bases of this chapter. It has been found that sales and marketing functions do not always align their activities but that they can improve their relationships if they collaborate over various marketing and customer acquisition processes, including the sales funnel, the development of the value proposition, gathering market intelligence and planning new product launches. How customers are acquired and retained (customer loyalty) will be reviewed, including through the customer journey, where we will consider customer touch points and how these can be assisted by social media. We will also explore the latest research into the contributions that sales can make to marketing intelligence and how marketing and sales can develop customer information so that senior managers can produce agile marketing strategies.

Why Consider Sales and Marketing Interactions?

The development of innovative and cohesive customer solutions requires cross-functional collaboration according to Chernetsky, Hughes and Schrock (2022), leading them to the proposition that of all the cross-functional relationships, the one between sales and marketing functions has the most impact on the bottom line. However, when these two organisational functions are operating correctly, they collectively identify and advance a potential customer from awareness to purchase, thereby contributing to the firm's ability to generate revenue and profit, and achieve other business goals (Hetenyi, 2020). In the absence of seamless cooperation between sales and marketing, marketing activities will be less effective and communications with the customer will not be integrated successfully with sales processes (Biemans, Malshe and Johnson, 2022; Järvinen and Taiminen, 2016). Marketing and sales misalignment has been estimated to have cost US businesses over $1 trillion annually (Hawthorne et al., 2019). It has been said that sales and marketing feud

DOI: 10.4324/9781003173892-3

almost as a matter of course, like Shakespeare's Capulets and Montagues, even though they are both customer-facing functions (Kotler, Rackham and Krishnaswamy, 2006). Where these departments are not satisfied with their interactions and relationship, there can be a negative effect on the business processes, including loss of prospective customers and existing customers, and building up excess inventories (Biemans, Malshe and Johnson, 2022). The relationship between sales and marketing functions has persisted as one of the major sources of organisational conflict due to the interactive nature of their relationship. They perform separate, but complementary activities to achieve the common goal of increasing revenues and profits (Cespedes, 1993; Kelemen-Erdős and Molnar, 2019).

The recommendation is that these functions should be encouraged to work together from the start of the selling process, exploring ideas on the presentation of the company's goods and services to the customer, having open conversations about the value proposition, sharing market intelligence and working jointly on marketing plans (Le Meunier-FitzHugh and Le Meunier-FitzHugh, 2015). Where sales and marketing work together on mutually beneficial projects such as launching new products and identifying qualified sales lead criteria together, there is less tension in the interface and fewer arguments in relation to the quality of the sales leads and marketing collateral. The creation of collaborating, cross-functional sales-marketing teams has been shown to have a positive effect on strengthening sales-marketing connections and internal relationships (Le Meunier-FitzHugh, Cometto and Johnson, 2021; Malshe, 2011).

Issues within Sales and Marketing Interactions

Having established that sales and marketing functions benefit from collaboration and that they are both customer facing, we should perhaps explore what are the issues of this internal interface. Research by Homburg and Jensen (2007) established there is evidence to support the view that Sales and Marketing teams rarely operate without a basic underlying conflict created by inconsistent objectives (short vs long term) and different thought worlds, which are the behaviours, beliefs and assumptions held by people working in similar roles and conditions (e.g., Malshe and Al-Katib, 2017). The contention is that this tension is necessary as sales and marketing have very different roles to perform, but that they also need to present an integrated, coherent view of the organisation's offer to customers. They need to be on the same page with regards to their understanding of the customer's changing needs and how they can satisfy them (Raymond, 2021).

In 1960, Theodore Levitt wrote in the Harvard Business Review that the differences between the sales and marketing functions are more than semantics. The sales' function plays a fundamental role within the organisation, which is selling goods or services directly to their customers (Blocker et al., 2012) in a way that meets the customers' needs. While marketing's main function is to create value for the customer by creating and communicating a product whose value is aligned with the needs of the buyer over a longer period of time (Hinson, Adeola and Amartey, 2018; Kotler, Rackham and Krishnaswamy, 2006). This process can be expensive, and it can be difficult to accurately measure the benefits of this expenditure. Consequently, sales are the organisation's revenue generating centre, while marketing is a cost centre. The challenge is that these roles and activities often overlap in a way that makes sales and marketing reciprocally interdependent, as they work in tandem to sell the organisations' product offering to customers (Hetenyi, 2020). The result can be that sales and marketing tend to experience ineffectiveness in the sales/marketing ecosystem that reduces the overall productivity of organisations (Hawthorne et al., 2019; Hughes, LeBon and Malshe, 2012). The lack of integrated goals and a clear delineation of roles and activities can contribute to the interface's problems. These fundamental differences may be further intensified if marketing feels that sales get the 'rewards' for achieving sales on the back of marketing's hard work, or if sales feel ignored in the planning of marketing activities that means that marketing collateral is not fit for sales use (Kelemen-Erdős and Molnar, 2019).

The sales function is close to the customer and is focused on tasks such as developing customer relationships, exploring pain points, making sales and delivering pre- and post-sales support. This focused information about the customer is vital to marketing, but it can only be valuable if it is shared in a way that is mutually beneficial and there are barriers to this happening, such as few incentives for salespeople to share information and no resources or systems for doing so (Chernetsky, Hughes and Schrock, 2022). Sales and marketing functions, therefore, operate with different timeframes and experience different ways of delivering value. Sales is a more continuous activity, customer-focused, relationship and results-oriented, while marketing is more project-based, brand-focused, process- and analysis-oriented (Malshe and Krush, 2020). Hetenyi (2020) highlighted the reality of sales and marketing's interdependence that requires clear lines of communication to enable them to engage in regular information exchanges, which can be difficult to achieve when salespeople are in a different location from marketing people and their different technical backgrounds may cause a communication/language gap between them.

These differences in perspective and operations between the sales and marketing functions create cooperation barriers that do vary from company to company, as well as industry to industry (Sleep, Lam and

Hulland, 2018). A study by Malshe, Johnson and Viio (2017) found that sales and marketing people experience dysfunction in the sales and marketing interface very differently. It was common for one party to indicate that the interface was working smoothly when their counterparts did not, so that some activities were identified as being dysfunctional by sales but were thought to be fine by marketing. Whatever the perceptions of the interface are, the presence of dysfunctional conflict appears to have a circular progression that could lead to either antitherapy or apathy towards the other function, and a reduction in flexibility and accommodation towards working together, which operates at all levels within the organisation, from marketing and salespeople to middle and even senior management (Malshe and Krush, 2020). It has been identified that the foundation of these impediments to sales and marketing cooperation varies at each level within the organisation. Senior sales and marketing managers are focused on the power to secure their own future advantage during strategy negotiations by trading on their ability to either sponsor or support the implementation of specific marketing projects. At the middle management level sales and marketing managers were found to be involved in a continuous wrangle for finite marketing mix resources, while on the frontline sales and marketing personnel were focused on prioritising their own productivity and earning potential, rather than working jointly to achieve overarching strategic goals. To say that sales and marketing tension is set at the top and trickles down through the business, is to state the obvious but these studies identify how this concept operates within the sales and marketing interface (Malshe and Krush, 2020; Malshe et al., 2021).

Strategies that can Facilitate Sales and Marketing Cooperation

There have been many suggested actions/levers made to help improve the sales and marketing interface. Contemporary research has identified a combination of organisational and communication-related levers that should be helpful in aligning activities. Organisational levers include job rotation, formal and informal meetings, cross-functional training, establishing cross-functional project teams and shared rewards (e.g., Le Meunier-FitzHugh, Piercy and Massey, 2011). The communication-related category includes creating a shared vision, unifying culture, sharing resources, aligned goals and trust (Johnson and Boeing, 2016; Kelemen-Erdős and Molnar, 2019) so these elements are also important in creating sales and marketing collaboration. Research has also confirmed that when management works to improve the sales and marketing interface, the two functions work well together and there is a positive impact on the organisation's performance (Le Meunier-FitzHugh and Piercy, 2007; Malshe, Johnson and Viio, 2017).

The key to aligning this interface appears to be to recognise that sales and marketing people bring different strengths to the revenue generation process and that when they are collaborating, they can exceed the sum of their parts. Collaboration may be created through formal and information interactions, and through interactive tools (Chernetsky, Hughes and Schrock, 2022). Malshe and Krush (2020) found that addressing the conflicting motivations and perspectives that create paradoxes in the sales and marketing interface will require a multilevel approach. Senior management need to generate a collaborative attitude to support the implementation of selected marketing strategies. The use of inclusive language to highlight mutual benefits, such as 'supporting this action would help us to achieve X', or visibly sharing the credit for success. The ability to agree targets and engaging in regular exchanges of information, allows sales and marketing to increase and complement each other's capacity to achieve (Le Meunier-FitzHugh, Cometto and Johnson, 2021). Using mutually inclusive language does, however, require trust, commitment, and perceived fairness between the two groups that can be difficult to obtain when there is a perceived dysfunction (Hetenyi, 2020).

Agreeing how resources will be allocated to different projects at the senior level (including contingency budgets) and using them flexibly during project implementations can help to reduce sales and marketing tension. For example, the regular injection of resources to specific projects such as targeting critical sales territories, or the promotion of specified brands, can help to reduce the negative effects of marketing resource battles (Malshe et al., 2021). Senior management plays a vital role in shaping collaborative sales and marketing relationships, but in international enterprises they also need to pay attention to any differences in national culture that can impact on internal processes, norms and behaviours. It has been found that the management of the sales and marketing interface needs not only to generate collaboration but is also required to establish flexibility over the use and exchange of resources, as well as being able to coordinate the use of those resources and knowledge (Dewsnap et al., 2020).

At the middle management level (sales management and marketing management), it has been found to be beneficial to set up formal, regular meetings to exchange information and listen to each other's ideas (Malshe and Krush, 2020). If management can facilitate information exchanges between sales and marketing, especially in the early stages of a marketing/sales campaign they can create cooperation, empathy and trust over the messages that need to be conveyed to the market (Le Meunier-FitzHugh, Cometto and Johnson, 2021). It has been noted that where there is no agreement or discussion, each manager becomes more entrenched in the idea that their own perception of the situation has the greatest value and becomes more defensive of their position. However, these opposing perspectives can become complementary with discussion and agreement between the parties on common goals, as well as sharing kudos and rewards (Malshe et al., 2021). Establishing formal and informal networks to promote information exchange and joint decision making is essential to improving the sales and marketing interface at this level in the organisation. Setting up opportunities for formal and informal exchanges aimed at solving a problem or exchanging information can create trust and greater productivity (Le Meunier-FitzHugh, Cometto and Johnson, 2021).

It is at the marketing/salesperson level that there is the greatest work to be done because it is where sales and marketing activities are in the greatest opposition and the most compromise is required. Open dialogue and mutual respect and trust provide a better chance of marketing strategies being successful whilst allowing salespeople the freedom of execution that they require. Sharing objectives and knowledge and agreeing upon a common accountability forms the foundation for a healthier sales and marketing interface (Malshe et al., 2021). Informal networks created between sales and marketing people can help them to understand the market and create agile marketing plans (Malshe and Krush (2020). However, changing the organisations' perception of the sales and marketing interface requires managers to embrace the paradox of their operations so that they can manage the inherent tensions and create synergy through collaboration. There is a critical need to develop flexible, cross-functional resource exchanges between sales and marketing in turbulent environments to enable them to deliver key business outcomes (Dewsnap et al., 2020). Setting up cross-functional project teams is recommended to be one way of achieving sales and marketing collaboration (Le Meunier-FitzHugh and Massey, 2019).

Collaborating to Enhance Market Intelligence

Market intelligence or knowledge consists of data generated through a system of research and synthesis that enables the organisation to gain competitive advantage and understand how to deliver customer value. Generating marketing intelligence is critical to informing marketing strategies and positively influences cross-functional collaboration related to decision making and collaboration (Le Meunier-FitzHugh and Piercy, 2006; Le Meunier-FitzHugh and Massey, 2019). Customer knowledge, information on industry trends and competitor information are all required in marketing and selling situations. One benefit of using social media as an information source is that it generates a wealth of customer information that can be analysed through media sites such as Google Analytics and Facebook Insights (Singh et al., 2019). The essential part of generating customer intelligence from digital sources is that it needs to be shared between sales and marketing personnel so that they can jointly craft the most suitable value proposition for the customer and potential customer. Metadata from big data streams are merged with information from salespeople to generate customer knowledge and identify trends and buying habits, so that appropriate customer value is created. Further, live feedback from customers allows the organisation to integrate the information with their intellectual capital to innovate and customise their offer to the customer.

Generating customer knowledge is an essential asset for the organisation in their quest to improve their products/offer and generate customer value (Chaithanapat and Rakthin, 2020). Providing this critical source of information is largely the responsibility of salespeople, but the flow of information from sales to marketing and senior management needs to be established through effective structures and processes. The rapid evolution of markets in both emerging and established markets is driving the need for customer knowledge to be rapidly formed through the marketing/sales interface. Generating this learning through internal/ external networks can promote rapid sensemaking and nimbleness in formulating marketing strategies to create customer value. Informal relationships and networks aid the speed of the flow of information to disseminate information (and stories) to develop action plans that can also reduce sales and marketing tensions (Malshe et al., 2021).

Collaboration in New Product Launches

It has been found that frequent formal and information meetings focused on achieving specific project objectives, such as creating plans for launching new products resulted in greater collaboration and positive relationships between sales and marketing people (Cometto et al., 2016). Interacting during launch plans for new products helped to build frequent information exchanges and trust between sales and marketing teams that resulted in higher-than-average sales for the new product group (Le Meunier-FitzHugh, Cometto and Johnson, 2021). However, the conceptualisation of each new product launch strategy will also be dependent on (1) the complexity of the new product, (2) whether the marketplace is developed or developing and (3) the effectiveness of Sales and Marketing interactions (Malshe and Biemans, 2014).

Promoting internal collaboration through each of the various stages of new product development was also identified as a critical knowledge transformation mechanism (Hirunyawipada, Beyerlein and Blankson, 2010). However, at the final stage of the product launch is when the integration of the market information from salespeople is critical to the launch success in the territory so that the customers' voice is 'heard' and incorporated into the launch plans. Consequently, to design successful launch plans it is necessary to empower sales and marketing teams to interact freely, exchange information and trust each other's expertise, so that customers are attracted to the new offerings (Le Meunier-FitzHugh, Cometto and Johnson, 2021). It is the responsibility of the senior management team to encourage formal, cross-functional planning meetings between sales and marketing to promote both formal and informal exchanges of information (Malshe et al., 2021). Information sharing in the planning process generates learning and mutual trust between sales and marketing teams. Trust in each other's knowledge and skills is a key factor in building relationship effectiveness that can generate learning and social exchanges that are beneficial to both parties, improving sales and marketing collateral (Le Meunier-FitzHugh, Cometto and Johnson, 2021). The need for managers to listen to market information from sales teams has been accelerated during the recent pandemic that has resulted in rapid changes in demand for fast-moving consumer goods (FMCG) and consumer products, as well as disruptions to the supply chain. The FMCG firms that are succeeding are those that listen attentively to consumers and move fast to bring solutions and appropriate product messages to their markets.

Collaborating in Customer Acquisition and the Customer Journey

Pipelines are a flow of opportunities going through various stages of a process where some of them will be removed, while others may successfully be won from the prospects. Companies looking to increase revenues and add new customers will find it difficult to achieve this goal successfully without a proper sales pipeline process. Pinpointing prospects helps increase the sales pipeline (Figure 3.1). This sales pipeline starts at the top where initial opportunities are reviewed and where appropriate, these are moved to qualified leads. These are reviewed and some of them become warm leads. The aim is to convert these warm leads into sales proposals and eventually some of these proposals will convert into actual new customers and sales. It is very important to have a qualified pipeline management system in place (Hughes, 2013). The pipeline can help determine what opportunities exist and what needs to be done to convert them into sales. It is essential when project work is being qualified into the sales pipeline that the company has the resources to deliver the project to meet the agreed deadlines of the customer. Poor revenue results can be attributed to low prospecting and bad pipeline development activity. If there is no pipeline then this will eventually lead to the premature death of the organisation (Etherington, 2010).

Managing the sales pipeline, or sales funnel is one of the principal activities of sales and marketing. Consequently, attracting and acquiring

Figure 3.1 The Sales Pipeline Activities.
Source: Created by Sheahan, 2020.

new customers and managing the customer journey to purchase is another area where sales and marketing collaboration can lead to greater financial benefits. The overall aim is to create, locate and convert customers to the organisation's offer. Traditionally marketing has managed the 'front-end' of this process by creating content on media sites (online and off-line) that should attract potential customers and engaging them with appropriate offers, while sales has been responsible for the 'back-end' or developing the 'lead' (interactions with the potential customer) so that they eventually purchase the offer (Malshe and Biemans, 2014). This two-step process provides plenty of areas of potential conflict between sales and marketing. For example, if the marketing department is responsible for creating a 'buzz' about the organisation's activities through marketing communications to locate and 'qualify' leads (identifying those potential new customers that have the ability/wish to purchase), which are then 'handed-on' to the sales department to 'close' (make a sale), when is the lead properly 'qualified'? When should the lead be handed-on? Which can result in accusations of mismanagement of the pipeline or even deliberate inaction by both parties. Salespeople's ability to follow up on new customer leads (self-generated and marketing generated) will depend on their motivation (if the leads are pre-qualified and managerially supported), opportunity (quantity of leads generated) and their individual ability (combination of experience and past performance). Many prospective leads maybe 'lost' if the hand-over is not clearly supported, or when salespeople do not have the right conditions or capacity to explore them (Sabnis et al., 2013).

Many organisations would benefit from establishing effective processes for including sales in customer acquisition as they provide opportunities for marketing to gain information from sales from the beginning of the pipeline and allowing sales to engage in the interaction with the customer at the appropriate moment, not just at hand-on (Malshe and Biemans, 2014). By incorporating input from the sales team, marketing can move the customer seamlessly through the entire buying cycle to purchase, which means that the customers' journey is not interrupted by a 'handover' (Le Meunier-FitzHugh and Le Meunier-FitzHugh, 2015). More and more organisations recognise the symbiotic relationship of sales and marketing over the management of the sales pipeline (Malshe and Krush, 2020). It has been identified that it is possible to create 'field marketing' roles that are specifically responsible for liaising with sales operatives to fill the sales pipeline. Salespeople have a valuable contribution to add to the customers' journey and to the design of content of webinars and case studies, as well as providing feedback to marketing about the market conditions and where to find new sales leads.

Sales Pipeline Execution Process (SPEP)

Sales being the lifeblood of all companies (Moncrief, Bedford and Bedford, 2017), but research has shown the front end of the sales process is under resourced (Virtanen, Parvinen and Rollins 2015). These early stages of the sales process are worthy of investigation as this concern of how to find and obtain new customers. The traditional seven steps of selling highlighted by Moncrief and Marshall (2005) have been reviewed (e.g., Arli, Bauer and Palmatier, 2018) and a gap has been identified in the early stages of customer acquisition leading to a loss of prospects, unqualified leads, and underdeveloped customer value propositions (CVP). Where organisations have the opportunity to start early relationships with potential new customers, they can build a stronger sales pipeline (Borg and Young, 2014). Research undertaken to investigate this front end of the sales pipeline has identified that sales need to work more closely with marketing (Sheahan, 2020). The SPEP (see Figure 3.2) framework has been developed to provide a process where sales and marketing are able to cooperate, share data and build relationships with prospects leading to strong trust and commitment between prospects and sellers. SPEP provides marketing and salespeople with a formal process for winning new customers, and which can also be used by management to drive revenues for both new and existing customers. Moving through each stage of the SPEP process can help achieve successful relationships with prospects in addition to acting as a framework in helping companies manage their sales pipeline effectively.

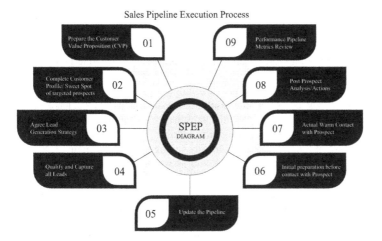

Figure 3.2 Sales Pipeline Execution Process (SPEP).
Source: Sheahan, 2020.

The first key requirement of a SPEP implementation is to gain senior management buy in as new processes often needs to be driven top down (Osarenkhoe and Bennani, 2007). The SPEP should be presented in its entirety to the sales and marketing teams and detailed discussions constructed on each of the stages. The second stage focusses on value creation as this is the raison d'être of most organisations. Therefore, a compelling customer value proposition (CVP) (Woiceshyn and Falkenberg, 2008) should be developed to help build an early rapport with the prospects where the buyer is able to identify the value that the supplier is bringing to the relationship and help them with the decision to buy. Where marketing is active in the organisation they will need to sit down with sales and agree on the CVP together. As previously discussed, it is critical both marketing and sales work together on this as it can provide a more compelling CVP and help build a good rapport between the functions. By having these joint meetings, they are sharing knowledge and information with each other which can lead to improved collaboration (Le Meunier-Fitzhugh and Massey, 2019).

Lead Generation

Research has identified that there are three top routes to successfully generate sales leads, referrals (Chollet, Geraudel and Mothe, 2014), WOM (Gombeski et al., 2011) and LinkedIn (Oechsli, 2011). This is where the focus needs to be when it comes to lead generation strategy in the company. Marketing needs to work with sales in forming the right links to the prospects; therefore, meetings should be set up with members of the sales team to discuss the lead generation strategy including how to cover each of these three routes. Additionally, marketing people are able to track all customers that the organisation's employee interface with through the website. These contacts should be followed up and relationships with the prospects created as they can result in very successful qualified leads being generated and prevents potential sales leads getting lost in a black hole (Sabnis et al., 2013). Capturing and following up more sales leads is the key point of the SPEP process. Ideally having a CRM system in place that can help track potential leads should assist in this process, but it means that CRM systems need to be also open to marketing personnel (Rodriguez and Honeycutt, 2011; Sheahan, 2020). The key stakeholders in the sales pipeline need to meet to discuss the findings and tracking leads because it is essential in building the sales pipeline.

The next step in the SPEP process after prospects have been identified, the CVP completed and the pre-qualified leads have been submitted, is to contact the prospects. This step is usually allocated to salespeople (although it can also be achieved by marketing people) and they will need to be well prepared before they contact the prospect so they will need to have gathered lot of information before they make their first contact. The number one route to help with first contact was LinkedIn as there is a lot of information available both from a buyer and organisational perspective (Sheahan, 2020). Being prepared should help speed up the buying acquisition process. Toman, Adamson and Gomez (2017) identified that proactive prescriptive approaches by suppliers to potential customers increase the ease of purchase by 86% and lead to a 62% chance in closing the sale. When the salespeople are contacting the prospect, it is no longer seen as a cold call but more of a warm call. At times it is not easy to get through to the relevant buyer, but perseverance is key to make successful contact with the buyer. It is also important to capture all activities with prospects and to update the CRM systems to help with tracking. Actions will need to be followed up by the salespeople after the initial contact and the sales pipeline will need to be updated for each opportunity (Järvinen and Taiminen, 2016). Tracking leads through CRM systems will allow sales management to monitor progress and ensure they are all closed out.

Bradford, Johnston and Bellenger (2016) highlighted by having a better understanding of the issues that impact converting sales leads opportunities can help sales management in their forecasting. Part of the SPEP implementation plan allows management to meet on a regular basis with other stakeholders in the sales pipeline, such as salespeople, marketing, operations and finance, so that they can reviewed. The pipeline review can show how the opportunities are progressing and how close they are to finalising the sale with the prospect (Peterson, Rodriguez and Krishnan, 2011) and where appropriate corrective action can be taken to address any issues such as lost or poorly qualified leads.

Research has established the importance of building relationships early in the customer acquisition process with the buyers (Hughes, Le Bon and Rapp, 2013; Kaski, Niemi and Pullins, 2018) and how critical a role this plays for future business – not just for salespeople but also for the referrals emanating from the sales pipeline process. This brings a new dimension by stressing the criticality in building relationships with prospective customers at the early part of the front end of the sales process (Sheahan, 2020). The participants felt that this was key as it was a perfect opportunity to demonstrate to the prospect that they knew what they were doing by responding quickly to customer enquiries and that they could deliver on their commitments. They also acknowledged that building a sales relationship early in the process helped to build credibility and trust between the supplier and the buyer that would bode well for the future relationship and increasing sales. The research also highlighted that building trust (Kaski et al., 2017) with the prospect/customer was critical and without this trust no business or partnership would take place. Trust and commitment are key elements in achieving relationship benefits with the customer with the added dimension of seeking this early at the front end of the sales process (Le Meunier-FitzHugh, Cometto and Johnson, 2021). All participants felt that it was important to build up trust early with the prospect and to respond quickly to any requests they have (Salomonson, Aberg and Allwood, 2012). The issue of persistence and building trust fits well with the relationship aspect of B2B sales that is prevalent in the literature (Hughes, 2013; Wagner and Mai, 2015). Integrity also came across from the research as important especially when making commitments to the customers.

Salespeople who are engaged in both the acquisition and retention of customers must manage their most precious resource – time – by dividing their activities between generating and following up leads (acquisition) and managing relationships, upselling, and cross-selling (customer retention) and non-sales activates such as training, research, and paperwork (Sabnis et al., 2013). However, salespeople are usually rewarded for closing sales, but not for helping to build the pipeline or creating customer value propositions so management will need to consider creating appropriate reward processes for salespeople to encourage their engagement (Le Meunier-FitzHugh and Massey, 2019). Consequently, it is essential that sales and marketing managers are clear when their people should be focusing their attention on non-sales and non-marketing activities, such as populating the sales pipeline/funnel or creating posts. Therefore, it should not just be marketing who are involved in designing new product launches, attracting new customers, and engaging customers through social media links and other offline channels. Social media may be used by both sales and marketing people to generate and 'warm up' leads. Online sites are also used to guide potential customers to the organisation's website and assist them to engage with the offer, provide feedback and become supporters of the brand. If salespeople are included in the early stages of new customer contact through social media as well as through the website, they can gain insights into the customers' interests that will make it easier for them to engage with the customer appropriately and generate greater customer value (This will be explored further in Chapter 5).

Conclusion

In this chapter, we have considered the impact of the sales and marketing interface and the effects of them not sharing knowledge, expertise and resources. We identified that cross-functional, informal networks between management, sales and marketing enable the capture of value that also allows senior management to access and react to specific customer information rapidly. We also considered the importance of creating strategic flexibility where managing the interdependencies between sales and marketing functions have become important considerations in co-creating value for and with customers. Flexible cross-functional resource exchanges between marketing and sales have positive performance and relationship outcomes, especially when the organisation is working within turbulent environments. We presented the SPEP framework for the front end of the sales process to enable marketing and salespeople win new customers and increase revenues. Extant research has found that organisations have become more strategic in managing their sales and marketing interface, leading to marketing function being pulled more towards creating and delivering customer value rather than marketing from a distance and sales becoming more involved in traditional marketing activities. This may result in the boundaries between sales and marketing functions becoming eroded and redefining the sales and marketing interface once again.

References

Arli, D., Bauer, C., and Palmatier, W. R. (2018). Relationship selling: Past, present and future. *Industrial Marketing Management*, 69, 169–184.

Biemans, W., Malshe, A., and Johnson, J. S. (2022). The sales-marketing interface: A systematic literature review and directions for future research. *Industrial Marketing Management*, 102, 324–337.

Blocker, C. P., Cannon, J. P., Panagopoulos, N. G., and Sager, J. K. (2012). The role of the sales force in value creation and appropriation: New directions for research. *Journal of Personal Selling and Sales Management*, 32 (1), 15–27.

Borg, W. S., and Young, L. (2014). Continuing the evolution of the selling process: A multi-level perspective. *Industrial Marketing Management*, 43 (4), 543–552.

Bradford, R. W., Johnston, J. W., and Bellenger, N. D. (2016). The impact of sales effort on lead conversion cycle time in a business-to-business opportunity pipeline. Paper presented at the 6th International Engaged Management Scholarship Conference.

Cespedes, F. V. (1993). Coordinating sales and marketing in consumer goods firms. *Journal of Consumer Marketing*, 10 (2), 37–55.

Chaithanapat, P., and Rakthin, S. (2020). Customer knowledge management in SMEs: Review and research agenda. *Knowledge and Process Management*, 28 (1), 71–89.

Chernetsky, V. V., Hughes, D. E., and Schrock, W. A. (2022). A synthesis of research on the marketing-sales interface (1984–2020). *Industrial Marketing Management*, 105, 159–191.

Chollet, B., Geraudel, M., and Mothe, C. (2014). Generating business referrals for SMEs: The contingent value of CEOs social capital. *Journal of Small Business Management*, 52 (1), 79–101.

Cometto, T., Nisar, A., Palacios, M., Le Meunier-FitzHugh, K., and Labadie, G. J. (2016). Organisational linkages for new product development: Implementation of innovation projects. *Journal of Business Research*, 69 (6): 2093–2100.

Dewsnap, B., Micevski, M., Cadogan, J. W., and Kadic-Maglajlic, S. (2020). Flexibility in marketing and sales interfacing processes. *Industrial Marketing Management*, 91, 285–300.

Etherington, B. (2010). *Cold Calling for Chickens* (Second ed.). London: Time Publishing Limited.

Gombeski, W., Britt, J., Wray, T., Taylor, J., Adkins, W., and Riggs, K. (2011). Spread the word. Word of mouth is a powerful, but often undervalued, marketing strategy—here's how to harness it. *Marketing Health*, 31 (1), 22–25.

Hawthorne, A., Miller, J., Sait, S., and Young, C. (2019). *101 B2B marketing and sales tips from The B2B Lead*. https://adindex.ru/files2/access/2013_11/104467_b2blead-marketing-sales-alignment-ebook.pdf. (Accessed: January 12, 2022).

Hetenyi, G. (2020). New research methods of sales-marketing interfaces. *International Journal of Engineering and Management Sciences*, 5 (3), 160–183.

Hinson, R., Adeola, O., and Amartey, A. F. O. (2018). *Sales Management: A Primer for Frontier Markets*. Charlotte, NC: Information Age Publishing Inc.

Hirunyawipada, T., Beyerlein, M., and Blankson, C. (2010). Cross-functional integration as a knowledge transformation mechanism: Implications for new product development. *Industrial Marketing Management*, 39 (4), 650–660.

Homburg, C., and Jensen, O. (2007). The thought worlds of marketing and sales: which differences make a difference? *Journal of Marketing*, 71 (3), 124–142.

Homburg, C., Jensen, O., and Krohmer, H. (2008). Configurations of marketing and sales: A taxonomy. *Journal of Marketing*, 72 (2), 133–154.

Hughes, D. E., Le Bon, J., and Malshe, A. (2012). The marketing–sales interface at the interface: creating market-based capabilities through organisational synergy. *Journal of Personal Selling & Sales Management*, 32 (1), 57–72.

Hughes, D. E., Le Bon, J., and Rapp, A. (2013). Gaining and leveraging customer-based competitive intelligence: the pivotal role of social capital and salesperson adaptive selling skills. *Journal of the Academy of Marketing Science*, 41 (1), 91–110.

Hughes, T. (2013). *The Joshua Principle* (3rd ed.). New South Wales: CIP Australia.

Järvinen, J., and Taiminen, H. (2016). Harnessing marketing automation for B2B content marketing. *Industrial Marketing Management*, 54, 164–175.

Johnson, J. S., and Boeing, R. (2016). A uniao faz a forca: (There is strength in unity): Understanding the sales–marketing interface in Brazil. *Journal of Personal Selling and Sales Management*, 36 (2), 190–205.

Kaski, T. A., Hautamaki, P., Pullins, E. B., and Kock, H. (2017). Buyer versus salesperson expectations for an initial B2B sales meeting. *Journal of Business and Industrial Marketing*, 32 (1), 46–56.

Kaski, T., Niemi, J., and Pullins, E. (2018). Rapport building in authentic B2B sales interaction. *Industrial Marketing Management*, 69, 235–252.

Kelemen-Erdős, A., and Molnar, A. (2019). Cooperation or conflict? The nature of the collaboration of marketing and sales organisational units. *Economics and Culture*, 16 (1), 58–69.

Kotler, P., Rackham, N., and Krishnaswamy, S. (2006). Ending the war between sales and marketing. *Harvard Business Review*, 84 (7–8), 68–78.

Le Meunier-FitzHugh, K., and Le Meunier-FitzHugh, L. C. (2015). *Creating Effective Sales and Marketing Relationships*. Business Expert Press.

Le Meunier-FitzHugh, K., and Massey, G. R. (2019). Improving relationships between sales and marketing: The relative effectiveness of cross-functional coordination mechanisms. *Journal of Marketing Management*, 35 (13–14), 1267–1290.

Le Meunier-FitzHugh, K., and Piercy, N. F. (2006). Integrating marketing intelligence sources. *International Journal of Market Research*, 48 (6), 699–716.

Le Meunier-FitzHugh, K., and Piercy, N. F. (2007). Does collaboration between sales and marketing affect business performance? *Journal of Personal Selling and Sales Management*, 27 (3), 207–220.

Le Meunier-FitzHugh, K., Massey, G. R., and Piercy, N. F. (2011). The impact of aligned rewards and senior manager attitudes on conflict and collaboration between sales and marketing. *Industrial Marketing Management*, 40 (7), 1161–1171.

Le Meunier-FitzHugh, K., Cometto, T., and Johnson, J. (2021). Launching new global products into subsidiary markets: the vital role of sales and marketing collaboration. *Thunderbird International Business Review*, 63 (4), 1–16.

Levitt, T. (1960). Marketing myopia. *Harvard Business Review*, 38 (4), 24–47.

Malshe, A. (2011). An exploration of key connections within the sales-marketing interface. *Journal of Business and Industrial Marketing*, 26 (1), 45–57.

Malshe, A., and Al Katib, J. (2017). A repertoire of marketers' trust-building strategies within the sales-marketing interface. *Journal of Personal Selling and Sales Management*, 37 (3), 213–227.

Malshe, A., and Biemans, W. (2014). The role of sales in NPD: an investigation of the U.S. health-care industry. *Journal of Product Innovation Management*, 31 (4), 664–679.

Malshe, A., Hughes, D. E., Good, V. and Friend, S. B. (2021). Marketing strategy implementation impediments and remedies: A multi-level theoretical framework within the sales-marketing interface, *International Journal of Research in Marketing*, 39 (3), 824–846.

Malshe, A., Johnson, J. S., and Viio, P. (2017). Understanding the sales-marketing interface dysfunction experience in business-to-business firms: A matter of perspective. *Industrial Marketing Management*, 63, 145–157.

Malshe, A., and Krush, M. T. (2020). Tensions within the sales ecosystem: A multi-level examination of the sales-marketing interface. *Journal of Business and Industrial Marketing*, 36 (4), 571–589.

Moncrief, W., Bedford, A., and Bedford, C. (2017). Are sales as we know it dying … or merely transforming. *Journal of Personal Selling & Sales Management*, 37 (4), 271–279.

Moncrief, W. C., and Marshall, G. W. (2005). The evolution of the seven steps of selling. *Industrial Marketing Management*, 34 (1), 13–22.

Oechsli, M. (2011). Using LinkedIn as a Prospecting Tool. *The Practice*, 80.

Osarenkhoe, A., and Bennani, E. A. (2007). An exploratory study of implementation of customer relationship management strategy. *Business Process Management Journal*, 13(1), 139–164.

Peterson, R., Rodriguez, M., and Krishnan, V. (2011). CRM and sales pipeline management; Empirical result for managing opportunities. *Journal of Marketing Management*, 21(1), 60–70.

Raymond, K. (2021). Are your marketing and sales teams on the same page? Harvard Business Review. https://hbr.org/2021/12/are-your-marketing-and-sales-teams-on-the-same-page. (Accessed: 30/07/2022).

Rodriguez, M., and Honeycutt, D. E. (2011). Customer Relationship Management (CRM)'s impact on B to B Sales Professionals' Collaboration and Sales Performance. *Journal of Business-to-Business Marketing*, 18 (4), 335–356.

Sabnis, G., Chatterjee, S. C., Grewal, R. and Lilien, G. L. (2013). The sales lead black hold: On sales reps' follow-up of marketing leads. *Journal of Marketing*, 77 (1), 52–67.

Salomonson, N., Aberg, A., and Allwood, J. (2012). Communication skills that support value creation. *Industrial Marketing Management*. 41 (1), 145–155.

Sheahan, K. (2020). Developing and Empirically Testing a Sales Pipeline Execution Process Framework. PhD Thesis. Technological University, Dublin.

Singh, J., Flaherty, K., Sohi, R. S., Deeter-Schmelz, D., Habel, J., Le Meunier-FitzHugh, K., Malshe, A., Mullins, R. and Onyemah V. (2019). Sales profession and professionals in the age of digitization and artificial intelligence technologies: concepts, priorities, and questions. *Journal of Personal Selling and Sales Management*, 39 (1), 2–21.

Sleep, S., Lam, S. K. and Hulland, J. (2018). The sales–marketing integration gap: a social identity approach. *Journal of Personal Selling and Sales Management*, 38 (40), 371–390.

Toman, N., Adamson, B., and Gomez, C. (2017). The new sales imperative. *Harvard Business Review*, 95 (2), 118–125.

Virtanen, T., Parvinen, P., and Rollins, M. (2015). Complexity of sales situation and sales lead performance: An empirical study in business-to-business company. *Industrial Marketing Management*, 45, 49–58.

Wagner, A. J., and Mai, E. (2015). What are they thinking? Establishing seller credibility through sales presentation strategy. *International Journal of Sales, Retailing and Marketing*, 4 (6), 3–17.

Woiceshyn, J., and Falkenberg, L. (2008). Value creation in knowledge-based firms: Aligning problems and resources. *Academy of Management Perspectives*, 22 (2), 85–99.

4 Sales Leadership and Customer Relationship Management (CRM)

Introduction

In the extremely competitive marketplace of the 21st century sales organisations are under a lot more pressure (Longenecker and Mallin, 2019). Research into sales leadership highlights that the sales leader is now required to manage complex customer portfolios and inspire flexible sales teams to deliver the performance required to fulfil their organisation's objectives effectively. Consequently, this chapter will not consider the traditional sales management topics of territory management, sales discipline and negotiation training, but will focus on what sales leaders will need to do to adapt to this changing landscape. A survey in the UK highlighted that 45% of buyers look to make their buying decisions remotely (The Rain Group, 2022). Salespeople will need leadership and training to develop new sales methods/patterns and strike a balance between virtual and traditional sales activities and sales leaders worldwide have recognised that a large part of their existing salesforce will require significant reskilling and organisations who do not provide sales training will fall behind (McKinsey, 2022). To help sales leaders to become adaptive they can utilise customer relationship management systems (CRM) to provide immediate information about developing sales patterns and the allocation of resources. However, CRM systems are expensive in terms of money and the resources needed to implement them, and there is still some debate about how effective CRM systems really are. These topics will be discussed further in this chapter to help our understanding of how sales excellence can be achieved in the future.

Challenges in Sales Leadership and Management

The salespersons' role has changed significantly over the last 20 years and management need to implement the right tools to enable these new sales activities to be developed. Sales managers need to be aware of the changes taking place in sales in the competitive landscape and that this will affect the salespeople they employ in the future so that they can

DOI: 10.4324/9781003173892-4

respond to these changes (Longenecker and Mallin, 2019). The amount of information available to buyers and sellers today is enormous compared to the past. In this context, it is important to note that 39% of B2B buyers select a supplier according to the skills of the salesperson rather than price, quality or service features (Fogel et al., 2012) and so recruiting the right salespeople is essential for the organisation's success. Customers are gathering information through using websites, social media, targeted advertising, reviews and ratings on products and companies, influencers on social media and customer blogs, and therefore the value of the salesperson's visit is in the intangible elements they can bring to the meeting rather than just product knowledge. Sales teams will therefore need to be adaptive so they can provide a better service to their customers (Rangarajan et al., 2021), and be a lot more agile to meet their customer demands for greater value.

Sales leadership research has typically taken a leader-focused approach, investigating key questions from a top-down perspective. Yet considerable research outside sales has advocated a view of leadership that takes into account the fact that employees look beyond a single designated individual for leadership (Flaherty et al., 2012). The sales leadership role is one in which the leader must manage a network of simultaneous relationships and several types of sales manager relationship internally and externally. The sales manager as a 'network engineer' must manage these multiple relationships and information flows between them. Four types of social network relationships for sales managers have been proposed – those with senior management, with other sales managers (peer-to-peer ties), with salespeople, and with customers (Flaherty et al., 2012). Therefore, they need the ability to connect with external thought leaders and partners with other functions within the organisation to be able to deliver solutions to achieve organisational goals (Le Meunier-FitzHugh and Douglas, 2016). Social networking promotes learning, better use of resources and facilitates complex problem-solving to better serve clients. Sales leaders must communicate pertinent information about sales and customers across departments. What is more, these relationships and roles are indispensable in the sales process, so this most important role of the sales manager should not be limited to one or two lines of communication. Working in sales can be a lonely existence, so salespeople also needs to feel that they have a supportive structure around them, and they are included by the sales leader in the communication network (Piercy and Lane, 2009).

The adoption of technology in the sales management role has brought several benefits including helping sales managers to identify the customers who should be satisfied with the organisation's value-creation efforts and help to identify which sort of strategic relationships can be built with them (Dixon and Tanner, 2012). Technology can help sales managers understand their customers and analyse buying patterns to help salespeople respond appropriately to different sales situations. Using customer sales data and purchase order analysis from SFA and CRM systems enables sales leaders to predict when customers need to be contacted and what they want to buy, improving customer retention (Hansen et al., 2011). It is also possible to manage the sales teams through technology to communicate with salespeople remotely via teleconferencing facilities and to interact with members of their social network. Sales managers are able to work from anywhere through various devices and to track salespeople's performance in real time during the sales process (Moncrief, Marshall and Rudd, 2015).

Managing Virtual Selling Environments

The rapid development of the Internet has posed a more significant challenge to the traditional sales model (Bongers, Schumann and Schmitz, 2021). Salespeople no longer sell alone but through the cooperation of an entire department or team to obtain and complete orders. Therefore, it has become essential to clarify the interaction between the sales manager and the sales team and to coordinate their relationship on and offline. Working in the new sales landscape will require upskilling of existing and new salespeople. Technology has advanced in this area and salespeople need to understand and be fully aware of which technology tools they should embrace to help them to be more effective in selling (Rangarajan et al., 2021). Even though there are advances taking place in sales automation, not all sales processes can be automated including areas such as the personal selling interface. The sales processes that are not automated will need salespeople with the right skill sets and organisations will need to invest in these areas to ensure they have the required attributes (Sheth and Sharma, 2008) and that the salespeople are prepared to deal with buyers/organisations demanding more from them (Arli, Bauer and Palmatier, 2018).

Buyers are researching more online, and they are well informed today and they can research online in real time to review competitors along with current market pricing. With this new digital sales landscape, data can be a significant differentiator for the sales team. Sales managers see digital interactions as being two to three times more important to their customers than traditional sales interactions (McKinsey, 2022). The disruption created by the Covid-19 pandemic has accelerated the number of areas where sales teams need to adapt, such as increasing flexibility, deciding which part of the sales function can be insourced or outsourced, and adopting the use of technologies (Sharma and Sheth, 2010). A research study highlighted that many companies have not received any formal social media training which can be a significant benefit to increasing sales (Sheahan, 2020). Some managers have been slow to embrace social media and its use is not being driven from the top down (Giamanco and Gregoire, 2012). Despite the fact that social media is recognised as central to the front end of the B2B sales process, this lack of management attention is mainly due to work overload and/or not having the budget to invest in social media. The investment cost can be prohibitive, and it is difficult for organisations to achieve a fast Return on Investment because it doesn't necessarily mean an increase in revenues result from investing in social media (Agnihotri et al., 2017).

Inside sales teams operating online can manage telemarketing programs, provide customer service support and can also engage in sales-related activities previously handled by outside salespeople (Rapp and Panagopoulos, 2012). The nature of inside sales has shifted, increasing in autonomy, importance and scope which supports the contention that inside sales will play a more active role in the future of sales (Syam and Sharma, 2018) and companies will need to ensure they hire the right salespeople with the correct set of sales skills to support this trend. Inside salespeople have a greater reliance on sales technology and data than outside salespeople (Sleep et al., 2020). Inside-sales represents the sales model of the digital era (Chaker et al., 2022) and with the right training, salespeople can use it to their advantage with prospects and customers. The activities of inside-sales teams can include supporting internal and external clients. Some of these activities handled by the inside-sales team can help free up time-consuming administrative issues which helps give the outside salespeople time to become more strategic in orientation with their customers (Sleep et al., 2020).

Managing data is now being recognised as a prerequisite for sales success and organisations are investing in CRM systems in an effort to collect and operationalise market/sales information. This requires sales managers to become proficient in these systems and in data analytics. Technology can also help sales managers with recruitment as candidates can participate in virtual interviews enabling them to demonstrate their ability to interact online. Further, more and more training can be delivered online, so that the sales manager can update their team. Recruitment and training the right salespeople are two of the most critical human resource decisions an organisation can make (Sullivan, Peterson and Krishnam, 2012), and may be seen as the single hardest task for managers (Cappelli, 2013), so it is essential that sales managers put time and effort into recruiting the right salespeople for the tasks in hand.

Recruitment

Effective recruitment and selection processes in sales are critical to organisations' continuing success as they facilitate survival, growth and innovation (Bolander et al., 2020). Without the right salespeople, the company will find it difficult to achieve their objectives (Piercy and Lane, 2009).

A shortage of sales skills has a negative impact on a company's achievement goals, thus it is important that a sales manager is responsible for recruiting potential personnel that fit the vacant position and enhancing their skills by a sales training programme. A sales manager's duty is to initially outline the skills and the expected expertise from the salesperson. The selection criteria for salespeople are frequently based on personal qualifications and attributes (Parravicini, 2015). Michael Watkins writing in Leadership (2022) identified that getting the right team in place to meet the needs of a rapidly moving market is critical. He was not talking about sales recruitment specifically but suggested that any team's composition should match the organisation's strategy and current situation. To achieve this, it is suggested that during recruitment the following questions should be considered when recruiting for the sales team:

- Are they an outstanding representative in their field?
- Do they have values that match those of the organisation?
- Can they balance what is good for their own benefit against the needs of the organisation?
- Do they really want to be here?
- Can they make their own decisions?
- Can they function as a member of this team?
- What roles could they play within the current team?

Recent research highlighted that the hiring of non-qualified salespeople can inhibit growth and the development and successful execution of the sales process, specifically within SMEs. The research showed that 75% of salespeople working in SMEs fell into sales with no sales experience or sales training (Sheahan, 2020). Several serious challenges that sales managers are facing around recruiting salespeople were identified are:

- We are hiring specialists and [expect to] retraining them.
- We have had to raise salaries to attract the best sales talent.
- We have no sales on-boarding programme.
- Sales is a maverick department; we can't be sure of what we are hiring.
- Sales is the only department without a learning and development programme.
- Our Employee Net Promoter Score is at an all-time low especially in sales.
- Sales staff attrition rate is close to 30%- we can't keep up.

Salespeople are motivated by money, but recent research has also shown that salespeople like working independently using their own initiative and have a desire to be financially successful, but they are also interested in job enrichment and career progression. These elements should be borne in mind when designing the recruitment process. Many organisations are outsourcing recruitment to more professional organisations who have experience of targeting the right sort of people, although just hiring the right person does not solve everything for the sales manager, as they also must fit into the team (Rapp and Panagopoulos, 2012).

Training

Before delving into sales training, it is worth noting that there is an accepted entry mechanism and educational path in many professions, but this is not the norm for sales. For example, few organisations will employ an accountant without an accounting qualification, a legal professional without a legal qualification, or a marketer without a marketing qualification, but there are few established qualifications for salespeople. As a result, many salespeople learn on the job and sales training is essential for growth and survival. In terms of sales training, more and more companies are designing systematic training programs for their employees generally, but this seldom extends to sales training (Lassk et al., 2012). While some of this oversight is due to the competing demands for budget, this lack of training may also be caused by a lack of awareness of the importance of a highly qualified sales team, despite some strong academic evidence of the benefits of sales training (Koponen, Julkunen and Asai, 2019). In 2020, 528 buyers were surveyed in relation to virtual selling and the results highlighted significant issues including, salespeople not being effective in relation to virtual selling, poor on listening, engagement, influencing buyers and not making the ROI clear to the buyer (Schmitz et al., 2020).

It is important that the awareness of sales team training is raised, especially around the various aspects of the sales process, the customer journey, value creation and use of technology. Since there has been a significant shift towards digital and social selling, salespeople need to be trained in this area to identify which techniques to use to aid their efforts (Hartmann et al., 2020). Specific selling skills such as adaptive selling behaviour, salesperson listening behaviour or rapport building (Gremler and Gwinner, 2008) are well known and can be targeted as appropriate, but as many as 80% of sales leaders identified analytical and quantitative skills as areas where salespeople need to develop their skills as high performing sales teams are 3.5 times more likely to use sales analytics than underperforming teams (Shahbaz et al., 2021). Organisations that are leveraging sales training are creating competitive advantages through initiating a successful prospecting program, clear value propositions and well-motivated sales teams can improve the organisation's overall performance (Lassk et al., 2012).

Buyers are moving from face-to-face meetings to virtual-based relationships. They can complete 70% of the customer journey before they even contact the supplier, so it is important the salespeople are trained to support this transition (Chaker et al., 2022). Salespeople need to be trained on how to respond to these virtual enquiries. They need to become virtual subject matter experts in each field as a rapid response is of the essence in the online sales process. Since there has been a significant shift towards digital selling salespeople need to be trained in this area. They also need to be developed in the area of social selling and which techniques to use which will aid their efforts (Hartmann et al., 2020). Since salespeople are heavily dependent on the effective use of social media to respond to these online elements, it is important that management allocate a budget for social media-related investments including training and sales enablement tools.

Research has confirmed that the motivation to receive virtual and social media training is very high among salespeople, sales managers and sales executives (Itani, Agnihotri and Dingus, 2017). Knowledge is power but despite having this power, buyers still need sellers to help them understand all the information at hand, and often they want to talk to a human sales representative. Salespeople need to be trained on how to reach these potential prospects quickly before the buyer makes their purchase decision through online sources (Guesalaga, 2016). Research has identified that sales mentoring has a positive effect on sales performance and if the mentoring is carried out internally it helps the salesperson to mimic the work behaviours of their mentors in similar work settings (Bradford, Rutherford and Friend, 2017). It is also suggested that sales training needs to be revised to include appreciation of the customers' role in value co-creation and shift the salesperson's perspective on what customer's value, especially when selling services where greater product knowledge is assumed (Baumann, Le Meunier-FitzHugh and Wilson, 2017). Organisations will need to establish what training programs and mentoring are required to ensure that their salespeople are able to compete in the marketplace and win new customers. To aid these developments organisations over a long period of time have tried to develop systems to help manage their customer portfolio. One of the most common systems that have been adopted are customer relationship management systems which has been shown to bring many benefits to the organisation.

Customer Relationship Management (CRM)

To manage the customer journey and the sales environment organisations have invested in CRM systems that are designed to help establish and build customer/client-business relationships. CRM has been defined as "the building of a customer-oriented culture by which a strategy is created for acquiring, enhancing the profitability of, and retaining customers, that is enabled by an IT application; for achieving mutual benefits for both the organisation and the customers" (Rababah, Mohd and Ibrahim, 2011: 223). In essence, the CRM software consolidates data collected on the customers' activities from all forms of communication into one digital place so that it can be analysed and cross-referenced. Therefore, CRM is a strategic software that allows the organisation to leverage customer data to increase the sales opportunities and to enhance customer satisfaction (Mariani, Perez-Vega and Wirtz, 2022). It is critical to strengthen connections with customers, suppliers, collaborators, partners and users, and the CRM platform can facilitate developing this customer orientation. The system records data from all sources, such as calls, emails, social media activity and online enquires, and it draws in and stores data on preferences highlighted in the client's communications. CRM technology facilitates salespeople in managing customer data, distinguishing customer values and prioritising on customers to enhance profits (Corsaro and D'Amico, 2022).

CRM systems help sales staff to record basic information about customers, the names of contacts and their potential purchasing activities. For example, in B2B business, due to the large number of people involved, sales staff can use the CRM system to record conversations with different people and identify the exact decision maker for an order by determining the customer's decision-making unit (DMU). However, there is a danger that salespeople will become over reliant on CRM systems (Wang and Feng, 2012) as salespeople are no longer required to remember the status of each customer. The use of CRM systems does help salespeople to be more efficient and reduce low-end repetitive operations. The information provided by this technology enables salespeople and sales managers to meet their customers' expectations with unity of direction, better time managements and efficiency. CRM also generates sales reports and forecasting to aid planning and decision making. Sales managers can also access performance information about their team to evaluate individual and team progress in meeting sales targets. CRM systems have the potential to create value between the selling organisation and its customers by managing and sharing information, thereby enhancing the relationships with customers and generating additional profits (Alshourah et al., 2022). This data can also be used by the marketing team to identify the latest trends and opportunities emerging in the market and facilitates in measuring the effectiveness of current marketing campaigns and formation of future campaigns (Anshari et al., 2019). With the use of CRM, sales personnel will have a 'single view of customer' no matter how customers contact business many companies use digital tools to increase effectiveness in selling and customer relationships management (Corsaro and D'Amico, 2022).

CRM is a tool to help a salesperson to gather/retain knowledge about their customers so that they can satisfy and retain them more effectively than operating without this information system. Organisations using CRM systems can understand their customer's needs in greater depth and are able to sell them the best possible solutions, which not only improves relationship with the customers but also generates more revenue for the organisation. Advanced CRM systems employ machine learning to understand customer behaviour and support customer acquisition, retention and profitability (Galitsky, 2020). Research has shown that organisations are heavily investing in CRM solutions because it can be five times more expensive to obtain a new customer than to retain an existing one (Wertz, 2018). CRM software not only understands buyer's behaviour through monitoring their online activities but also provides sellers with information on when to reach out to them. Salespeople use mixed-media touchpoints to collect and analyse customer data such as demographics and digital engagement (e.g., clicks, comments and shares) that is fed into the CRM systems to be cross-referenced with the customer's previous buying behaviour to cross-sell and up-sell in real-time, so that they can satisfy the needs of prospects or customers, based on preferences that are beneficial to both parties (Appointy, 2021).

CRM manages customer interaction throughout the customer life-cycle so that all data related to customer interactions are kept in one single location so that it can be interrogated. Research has shown that there is strong evidence that CRM adoption and implementation have a positive impact on sales performance, sales success and collaboration (Rodriguez and Honeycutt, 2011). The use of CRM allows salespeople improve collaboration with customers and build healthy customer relationships. It also increases their reach to include co-workers, supply chain partners and prospects (Moore, Raymond and Hopkins, 2015). CRM systems detail the activity levels of each customer, number of offers sent to the customers, orders placed, billings, open offers and this information is good for the salesperson to have when they are in dialogue with their customer, as it can help to guide their conversations. CRM also looks at the customers' orders and relates it to the company's sales force to gauge how well they are performing (Trainor et al., 2014). Research indicates that CRM systems when executed fully can reap significant benefits such as customer responsiveness, improved customer satisfaction, loyalty and retaining high-value customers which ultimately leads to higher revenues and profits and increasing customer lifetime value (CLV) along with improving the company's performance (Guerola-Navarro et al., 2021). Using CRM information to provide tailored value propositions for specific customers can add to customer satisfaction. It has also been found that where salespeople can demonstrate a deeper knowledge of their customers' business, they build both trust and customer confidence (Chonko, 2021).

Another significant benefit of employing CRM systems is in the improvement in call productivity of salespeople as they have a greater understanding of the markets operation and their own competitive advantage within those markets. Salespeople are said to spend up to 65% of their time on non-revenue-generating activities such as administrative tasks (Krogue, 2018) and this can be reduced through employing CRM systems. Software such has Salesforce, Zoho Corporation, HubSpot are examples of CRM technologies that are being used by the majority of the businesses worldwide. However, the challenge in practice is to identify how the sales team should implement CRM, as these techniques can be detrimental when salespeople find it difficult to access the systems or spend too much time uploading or checking data inputs. Salespeople understand that CRM has aided them in client tracking, outreach efforts, revenue tracking and customer analytics but some wish that CRM offered more facilities, such as automate lead qualification, automate data entry processes and recommended content to share with buyers. Cullen (2022) found that 80% of salespeople now find themselves working with data and data inputting more than talking to customers, which were traditionally marketing tasks, which raises the question of how beneficial CRM truly has been for the sales team. However, the debate continues to consider if CRM systems effectively reduce salespeople's work or simply just changed the way that they managed their customers.

Some studies have confirmed that the positive impacts of CRM on managing customer relationships, it still brings with them 'dark effects'. In fact, nearly 70% of implementations do not produce the expected benefits and many organisations are findings that implementing new CRM systems is creating 'technostress' in salespeople (Pullins, Tarafdar and Pham, 2020). Research finds that salespeople might value CRM systems more highly when they see the positive outcomes from their colleagues. Ease of use and system adaptability also contribute significantly to the acceptance of new systems (Mahlamäki et al., 2020). Therefore, it is suggested that sales managers should hire salespeople that can apply the use of CRM technologies in their daily activities and that they should put more effort into training salespeople to use technology tools to help them implement the tools well. CRM technologies and innovations are based on a customer-centric approach to the sales model. The objective is to maximise the revenue by focusing on meeting the customers' needs and increasing customer satisfaction through enhancing the customer experience and increasing their standard of service (Rangarajan et al., 2021).

Research found that despite companies seeing increasing demands from buyers, they are not using CRM to gain an advantage over their competition (Xuhua, Elikem and Worwui, 2019). Companies have electronic or manual systems in place for tracking sales leads and opportunities and they find this effective. They do not recognise the advantages in having a CRM system in companies even though it can help align sales activities and develop management control systems (Malek, Sarin and Jaworski, 2018). Research found that the findings did not support the literature on all the benefits of having a CRM system (Bradford, Rutherford and Friend, 2017; Hartmann, Wieland and Vargo, 2018). The data did not agree with the advice from academic papers that by having CRM processes in place the company can achieve better performance. Salespeople felt it was very costly, resource consuming, that not all salespeople were using it consistently. There was also some concern that CRM could create a Big Brother (Jelinek, 2013) effect. Research highlighted that where CRM was successfully implemented, it was successful in bringing in the salespeople at the development stage so that they could make their contributions and feel part of the internal process. The findings did support the literature that CRM implementation needs management support and involvement in order to execute it successfully (Ahani et al., 2017). Overall, a question mark still hangs over how effective a CRM system is in a company and as sales is working in this new post-Covid landscape further research will be required in this area.

There are significant advantages from integrating blockchain technology with CRM systems (Kinnett and Saeed, 2022). First, compared to traditional CRM that stores all the data on the cloud which makes it easy to access, blockchains require a key code to access the information. Consequently, blockchain can enhance the security of the data and it will no longer be necessary for organisations and customers to be concerned about their data being altered (Kuanar et al., 2022). Second, blockchain can reduce the amount of time and effort that is required to track information from the database by using unique codes. Finally, all transaction activity can be processed without the involvement of a third party, which reduces not only the time to usage but also the risk of data leakage (Kuanar et al., 2022). Although blockchain could be seen as a valuable tool for CRM, there are some disadvantages to it, specifically for those companies that are in the B2B sector as the transparency of the network might lead to less trust between the parties (Kinnett and Saeed, 2022).

Conclusion

This chapter covered the challenges of sales leadership and its changing landscape and a review of the use of CRM in the management process. We identify that sales management needs to give effective leadership in building adaptive sales teams to drive sales and meet customer demands. The importance of recruitment and sales training in building a successful sales team to meet these changes is discussed and highlights new technology management skills and agile practices are required for success. It is therefore critical for organisations to recruit people with the wide range skills that are required, and this can be achieved by either recruiting experienced salespeople or recruiting entry-level salespeople who have the ability to learn new skills and adapt to this challenging environment. Whichever route is chosen it is becoming essential that organisations have the processes in place to identify and develop appropriate talents.

Sales training can help to develop the attributes that each selling situation requires, but this alone is not sufficient to help sales managers adapt to the changes in technology that have been introduced. Salespeople are required to be adaptive and to embrace new technology. This is rarely successful unless support is put in place to ensure that the whole sales team can use and understand how technology can help them in their day-to-day job. CRM systems have been around now for several years and has been shown to be beneficial to organisations in managing their customer portfolio/customer journey. However, the effectiveness of CRM systems relies on a successful introduction, sales leaders need to understand the outputs, as well as the upskilling of salespeople. Therefore, sales training should not just be about improving sales skills, but should now also include the various usage of developing technologies, including social selling, which is playing a key role in meeting the needs of the new sales landscape, post Covid-19. Chapter 5 further explores digital selling and the use of AI in sales processes.

References

Agnihotri, R., Trainor, K. J., Itani, O. S., and Rodriguez, M. (2017). Examining the role of sales-based CRM technology and social media use on post-sale service behaviors in India. *Journal of Business Research*, 81, 144–154.

Ahani, A., Ab, Z., Nor, and Nilashi, M. (2017). Forecasting social CRM adoption in SMEs: A combined SEM-neural network method. *Computers in Human Behaviour*, 75, 560–578.

Alshourah, S., Jodeh, I., Swiety, I. and Ismail, A. (2022). Social customer relationship management capabilities and performance: moderating social media usage among Jordanian SMEs. *Decision Sciences*, 25(S2), 1–8.

Anshari, M., Almunawar, M. N., Lim, S. A., and Al-Mudimigh, A. (2019). Customer relationship management and big data enabled: Personalization and customization of services. *Applied Computing and Informatics*, 15(2), 94–101.

Appointy (2021). *How to Use Customer Data to Upsell More: A Definitive Guide for Business Owners*. Available from: https://blog.appointy.com/2021/02/12/use-customer-data-to-upsell-more/. (Accessed: November 12, 2022).

Arli, D., Bauer, C., and Palmatier, W. R. (2018). Relationship Selling, past, present and future. *Industrial Marketing Management*, 69, 169–184.

Baumann, J., Le Meunier-FitzHugh, K., and Wilson, H. N. (2017). The challenge of communicating reciprocal value promises: Buyer-seller value proposition disparity in professional services. *Industrial Marketing Management*, 64(7), 107–121.

Bolander, W., Satornino, C. B., Allen, A. M., Hochstein, B., and Dugan, R. (2020). Whom to hire and how to coach them: a longitudinal analysis of newly hired salesperson performance. *Journal of Personal Selling and Sales Management*, 40(2), 78–94.

Bongers, F. M., Schumann, J. H., and Schmitz, C. (2021). How the introduction of digital sales channels affects salespeople in business-to-business contexts: a qualitative inquiry. *The Journal of Personal Selling and Sales Management*, 41(2), 150–166.

Bradford, S., Rutherford, N. B., and Friend, B. S. (2017). The impact of training, mentoring and coaching on personal learning in the sales environment. *Journal of Personal Selling and Sales Management*, 15(1), 133–151.

Cappelli, P. (2013). Human resources for neophytes. *Harvard Business Review*, 91(10), 25–28.

Chaker, N. N., Nowlin, E. L., Pivonka, M. T., Itani, O. S., & Agnihotri, R. (2022). Inside sales social media use and its strategic implications for salesperson-customer digital engagement and performance. *Industrial Marketing Management*, 100, 127–144.

Chonko, L. B. (2021). *Advanced Introduction to Sustainable Competitive Advantage in Sales*. Cheltenham: Edward Elgar Publishing.

Corsaro, D., and D'Amico, V. (2022). How the digital transformation from COVID-19 affected the relational approaches in B2B. *Journal of Business and Industrial Marketing*, 37(10), 2095–2115.

Cortez, R. M., Johnston, W. J., and Dastidar, A. G. (2023). Managing the content of LinkedIn posts: Influence on B2B customer engagement and sales? *Journal of Business Research*, 155, 113388.

Cullen, M. (2022). *Sellers' roles have significantly changed—it's time their CRM software did to, Blogs.oracle.com*. Customer Experience Blog. Available at: https://blogs.oracle.com/cx/post/sellers-roles-have-significantly-changed-time-crm-software-did-too. (Accessed: November 12, 2022).

Dixon, L. A., and Tanner, F. J. (2012). Transforming selling: Why it is time to think differently about sales research. *Journal of Personal Selling and Sales Management*, 32 (1), 9–13.

Flaherty, K., Lam, S. K., Lee N., Mulki J. P., and Dixon A. L. (2012). Social network theory and the sales manager role: Engineering the right relationship flows. *Journal of Personal Selling & Sales Management*, 32(1), 29–40.

Fogel, S., Hoffmeister, D., Rocco, R., and Strunk, P. D. (2012). Teaching sales. *Harvard Business Review*, 91(5), 94–99.

Galitsky B. (2020). *Artificial Intelligence for Customer Relationship Management*; *Keeping Customers Informed*. Springer.

Giamanco, B., and Gregoire, K. (2012). Tweet me, friend me, make me buy. *Harvard Business Review*, 90(7/8), 88–93.

Gremler, D. D., and Gwinner, K. P. (2008). Rapport-building behaviors used by retail employees. *Journal of Retailing*, 84(3), 308–324.

Guerola-Navarro, V., Oltra-Badenes, R., Gil-Gomez, H., and Gil-Gomez, J. A. (2021). Research model for measuring the impact of customer relationship management (CRM) on performance indicators. *Economic Research-Ekonomska Istraživanja*, 34(1), 2669–2691.

Guesalaga, R. (2016). The use of social media in sales: Individual and organizational antecedents, and the role of customer engagement in social media. *Industrial Marketing Management*, 54, 71–79.

Hansen, J. D., Singh, T., Weilbaker, D. C., and Guesalaga, R. (2011). Cultural intelligence in cross-cultural selling: Propositions and directions for future research. *Journal of Personal Selling and Sales Management*, 31(3), 243–254.

Hartmann, N., Plouffe, C. R., Kohsuwan, P., and Cote, J. A. (2020). Salesperson influence tactics and the buying agent purchase decision: Mediating role of buying agent trust of the salesperson and moderating role of buying agent regulatory orientation focus. *Industrial Marketing Management*, 87, 31–46.

Hartmann, N. N., Wieland, H., and Vargo, L. S. (2018). Converging on a new theoretical foundation for selling. *Journal of Marketing*, 82(2), 1–18.

Itani, S. O., Agnihotri, R., and Dingus, R. (2017). Social media use in B2B sales and its impact on competitive intelligence collection and adaptive selling: Examining the role of learning orientation as an enabler. *Industrial Marketing Management*, 66, 64–79.

Jelinek, R. (2013). All pain, no gain? Why adopting sales force automation tools is insufficient for performance improvement. *Business Horizons*, 56(5), 635–642.

Jobber, D., Lancester, G., and Meunier-FitzHugh, K. (2019). *Selling and Sales Management* (11th ed.). Harlow: Pearson Education Limited.

Kinnett, S. J., and Saeed, A. (2022). When Blockchain Meets CRM: An Evaluation of Enterprise CRM Vendor Blockchain Capabilities. Available at: https://aisel. aisnet.org/amcis2022/sig_entsys/sig_entsys/1. (Accessed: November 12, 2022).

Koponen, J., Julkunen, S., and Asai, A. (2019). Sales communication competence in international B2B solution selling. *Industrial Marketing Management*, 82, 238–252.

Krogue, K. (2018). '*Why Sales Reps Spend So Little Time Selling*' [Online]. Available at: https://www.forbes.com/sites/kenkrogue/2018/02/15/why-sales-reps-spend-so-little-time-selling/?sh=aa0be6c1051b. (Accessed: October 23, 2022).

Kuanar, S. K., Mishra, B. K., Peng, S.-L., and Dasig, D. D. (2022). *The Role of IoT and Blockchain: Techniques and Applications*. Abingdon: CRC Press.

Lassk, G. F., Ingram, N. T., Kraus, F., and Mascio, D. R. (2012). The future of sales training; Challenges and related research questions. *Journal of Personal Selling and Sales Management*, 32(1), 141–154.

Le Meunier-FitzHugh, K., and Douglas, T. (2016). *Achieving a Strategic Sales Focus: Contemporary Issues and Future Challenges*. Oxford: Oxford University Press.

Longenecker, C. O., and Mallin, M. L. (2019). Key leadership skills of great sales leaders. *Development and Learning in Organisations*, 34 (3), 7–10.

Mahlamäki, T., Storbacka, K., Pylkkönen, S., and Ojala, M. (2020). Adoption of digital sales force automation tools in supply chain: Customers' acceptance of sales configurators. *Industrial Marketing Management*, 91, 162–173.

Malek, L. S., Sarin, S., and Jaworski, J. B. (2018). Sales management control systems: Review, synthesis and directions for future exploration. *Journal of Personal Selling and Sales Management*, 38(1), 30–55.

Mariani, M. M., Perez-Vega, R., and Wirtz, J. (2022). AI in marketing, consumer research and psychology: a systematic literature review and research agenda. *Psychology and Marketing*, 39(4), 755–776.

McKinsey and Company (2022). *The Imperatives for Automation Success, McKinsey and Company*. Available at: https://www.mckinsey.com/capabilities/operations/our-insights/the-imperatives-for-automation-success. (Accessed: November 15, 2022).

Mich, C. C., Conners, E. S., and Feldman, L. (2014). The impact of experiential learning on student perceptions of a career in sales. *Academy of Marketing Studies*, 18(2), 1–17.

Moncrief, W., Marshall, W. G., and Rudd, J. M. (2015). Social media and related technology: Drivers of change in managing the contemporary sales force. *Business Horizons*, 58(1), 45–55.

Moore, J. N., Raymond, M. A., and Hopkins, C. D. (2015). Social selling: A comparison of social media usage across process stage, markets, and sales job functions. *Journal of Marketing Theory and Practice*, 23(1), 1–20.

Parravicini, M. (2015). *A guide to Sales Management: A Practitioner's View of Trade Sales Organizations*. New York: Business Expert Press.

Piercy, N., and Lane, N. (2009). *Strategic Customer Management*. Oxford: Oxford University Press.

Pullins, E., Tarafdar, M., and Pham, P. (2020). The dark side of sales technologies: How technostress affects sales professionals, *Journal of Organisational Effectiveness: People and Performance*, 7 (3), 297–320.

Rababah, K., Mohd, H., and Ibrahim, H. (2011). A unified definition of CRM towards the successful adoption and implementation. *Academic Research International*, 1(1), 220–228.

The Rain Group, How to Sell through LinkedIn. Available at: https://www.rainsalestraining.com/blog/how-to-sell-through-linkedin. (Accessed: July 27, 2022).

Rangarajan, D., Sharma, A., Lyngdoh, T., and Paesbrugghe, B. (2021). Business-to-business selling in the post-COVID-19 era: Developing an adaptive sales force. *Business Horizons*, 64(5), 647–658.

Rapp, A. (2009). Outsourcing the sales process; Hiring a mercenary sales force. *Industrial Marketing Management* 38, 411–418.

Rapp, A., and Panagopoulos, N. G. (2012). Perspectives on personal selling and social media: Introduction to the special issue. *Journal of Personal Selling and Sales Management*, 32(3), 301–304.

Rodriguez, M., and Honeycutt, D. E. (2011). Customer Relationship Management (CRM)'s Impact on B-to-B Sales Professionals' collaboration and sales performance. *Journal of Business-to-Business Marketing*, 18(4), 335–356.

Schmitz, C., Friess, M., Alavi, S., and Habel, J. (2020). Understanding the impact of relationship disruptions. *Journal of Marketing*, 84(1), 66–87.

Schultz, M., and Doerr, E. J. (2014). *Insight Selling*. New Jersey: Wiley Publications.

Sharma, A., and Sheth, N. J. (2010). A framework of technology mediation in consumer selling: Implications for firms and sales management. *Journal of Personal Selling and Sales Management*, 30(2), 121–129.

Shahbaz, M., Gao, C., Zhai, L., Shahzad, F., Luqman, A., and Zahid, R. (2021). Impact of big data analytics on sales performance in pharmaceutical organisations: The role of customer relationship management capabilities. *PLOS ONE*, 16(4), p. e0250229.

Sheahan, K. (2020). Developing and Empirically Testing a Sales Pipeline Execution Process Framework. PhD Thesis. Technological University, Dublin.

Sheth, J. N., and Sharma, A. (2008). The impact of the product to service shift in industrial markets and the evolution of the sales organisation. *Industrial Marketing Management*, 37(3), 260–269.

Sleep, S., Dixon, A. L., DeCarlo, T., and Lam, S. K. (2020). The business-to-business inside sales force: Roles, configurations and research agenda. *European Journal of Marketing*, 54(5), 1025–1060.

Sullivan, Y. U., Peterson, M. R., and Krishnam, V. (2012). Value creation and firm sales performance; The mediating role of strategic account management and relationship perception. *Industrial Marketing Management*, 41, 166–173.

Syam, N., and Sharma, A. (2018). Waiting for a sales renaissance in the fourth industrial revolution: Machine learning and artificial intelligence in sales research and practice. *Industrial Marketing Management*, 69, 135–146.

Trainor, K. J., Andzulis, J. M., Rapp, A., and Agnihotri, R. (2014). Social media technology usage and customer relationship performance: A capabilities-based examination of social CRM. *Journal of Business Research*, 67(6), 1201–1208.

Wang, Y., and Feng, H. (2012). Customer relationship management capabilities: Measurement, antecedents and consequences. *Management Decision*, 50(1), 115–129.

Watkins, M. (2022). Why you must move fast to get the right team in place. *Leadership Journal*. Available from https://iby.imd.org/leadership/why-you-must-move-fast-to-get-the-right-team-in-place/. (Accessed: July 7, 2022).

Wertz, J. (2018). *Don't spend 5 times more attracting new customers, nurture the existing ones,* Forbes. Forbes Magazine. Available at: https://www.forbes.com/sites/jiawertz/2018/09/12/dont-spend-5-times-more-attracting-newcustomers-nurture-the-existing-ones/?sh=750107db5a8e. (Accessed: October 13, 2022).

Xuhua, H., Elikem, O., and Worwui, B. D. (2019). Effects of business e-commerce adoption on competitive advantage of small and medium sized manufacturing enterprises. *Economics and Sociology*, 12(1), 80–89.

5 The Future of Selling in a Virtual and Artificial Intelligence World

Introduction

The growth of virtual selling environments and sophisticated digital platforms are driving customer purchases online, and this is reconfiguring the sales process. Therefore, this chapter will build on the concepts of creating customer knowledge through sales technology, social media interactions, sales force automation and the use of artificial intelligence (AI) to manage customers and develop new sales communications and processes. Using social media as a selling tool is becoming the norm in sales practice, but its use presents sales teams with new challenges that are hard to ignore. For example, how to generate value through social media interactions is a major debate and research is also developing around how the sales team can be deployed effectively to build sales around the use of AI. We will explore research into how the sales team can move to virtual selling environments and using such technology as video conferencing, webinars, online meetings, social media and chatbots, whilst still developing customer trust and value.

Sales technology refers to the digital tools and services used by sales organisations to accelerate and facilitate sales productivity and sales processes to gain maximum sales output. The function of sales has become more digitalised over the past two decades and the increase of digital tools and technologies presents salespeople with new opportunities and challenges. Sales force automation, AI, augmented reality (AR), social media selling and other technologies are the new opportunities, and they are transforming sales activities and sales management practices (Singh et al., 2019). Sales technologies simply make the life of the sales department easier by removing the need for people to undertake repetitive, administrative tasks and by analysing big data thereby offering new opportunities for managing customer relationships. Sales technology mirrors information systems and communication technologies that are employed across the organisation to conduct its crucial activities. These technologies are changing the world of sales rapidly and

DOI: 10.4324/9781003173892-5

it is imperative that the companies can leverage them so that they can keep reinventing themselves and stay in touch with the global and local marketplaces. After all, change is the only constant in the business world and anything that helps to improve efficiency and effectiveness are very welcome.

Technology Enabling Sales

Research has identified technology as a key area of development in sales as it helps enable the sales process. Hunter and Perreault (2006:96) refer to sales technology as *"information technologies that can facilitate or enable the performance of sales tasks"*. Advances in technology and increasing customer demands are forcing organisations to review their information technology strategy to see how they can gain advantage over their competition. Technology is increasing the number of channels to market and providing digital paths for growth (Harrison and Hair, 2017). Technology includes the growing area of social media that is offering sales new communications channels and contact points with their customers (Cortez, Johnston and Dastidar, 2023). Organisations utilising digital sales channels will need to revaluate their sales team's activities and their sales processes (Singh et al., 2019). Research has shown that sales force automation (SFA) should help the organisation improve its sales performance by removing repetitive tasks allowing salespeople to focus on customer-orientated processes (Agnihotri et al., 2017; Corsaro, Maggioni and Olivieri, 2021). Sales automation and data analytics are offering sales teams increasingly accurate customer information. These tools and technologies have come together to create a new sales digital ecosystem that are shaping how customers interact with the buying and selling process (Rusthollkarhu, Hautamaki and Aarikka-Stenroos, 2020).

Sales Force Automation

SFA is the application of information technology that converts manual sales activities into an automated processes through software applications to improve efficiency and the optimisation of resources (Sanfilippo, 2022). The SFA is the broad automation of processes that aim to make them as efficient as possible, while CRM systems are more specific and help the sales teams to manage their relationships with customers by gathering data, tracking of buyer behaviours, following customer journeys and nurturing customer leads. Sales activities such as lead generation and prioritisation, collating information, processing orders, responding to customers, call logging and data entry (autofill) can be part of sales automation, which standardises activities and connects salespeople with other parts of the company (Zoltners et al., 2021). Sales teams are using software to manage the sales process more effectively. Sales technology enables organisations to analyse data to generate knowledge that provides salespeople with the ability to assess the best way to manage their interactions. For example, the development of electronic data interchange (EDI) systems can communicate with various customer management systems, such as ordering, delivery and inventory systems, customer databases and just-in-time (JIT) inventory systems thereby accelerating the exchange of information that may remove the need for individual sales visits (Corsaro, Maggioni and Olivieri, 2021). SFA systems enable improving generic salesforce functions by making sure that data about clients, accounts, goods, prices, technology, market trends, and institutional memory are effectively stored and shared. Research on sales practice and sales force automation has proven that automating processes is the future bases of increasing overall efficiency and effectiveness.

The aim of SFA systems is to leverage information technology to reduce errors and improve efficiency and provide the sales team with tools to manage customer information through the collection and synthesis of large amounts of information on customers and competitors. This technology not only helps the sales team to manage customer relationships, it also allows salespeople to improve their sales routine by automating repetitive sales processes such as selling, ordering, reporting, servicing, and consulting (Sanfilippo, 2022). SFA allows salespeople to free up time from back-office operations and focus more on revenue-generating tasks such as lead management, lead evaluation and prioritisation, and salespeople can then select prospects that are showing interest in the product and contact them. It has been suggested that SFA technology can effectively increase sales closure by 30%, shorten the sales cycles by around 18%, and lessening the time spent on administrative tasks by 14%. Moreover, the click-through rate on the website (CTR) can be improved by up to 152% (Troncoso, 2022). Many sales activities can be automated, follow-up contacts, meeting scheduling and sales reports and this solution frees up a salesperson's time by 15% to 20% whilst not compromising on sales conversion effectiveness (Sanfilippo, 2022). This integration of CRM and SFA, allows organisations to update the status of their leads, send emails automatically, and track customer engagement.

Three examples of SFA functions that have been identified as beneficial to sales are contact management, task management and pipeline management. Contact Management helps to track communications, interactions and activities between sales teams and customers. It collects and stores personal data and can connect with other automated tools to track customer behaviour and their journey through the website, which improves the customer experience and satisfaction (Corsaro, Maggioni and Olivieri, 2021). Task Management removes the necessity for salespeople to carry out routine tasks personally. Bishop (2020) explained that task-related technology helps salespeople make their activities more manageable by prioritising them in different ways, such as Critical, High, Medium or Low. Alternatively, a time-based system may be used such as Now, Today, Tomorrow, This week, and This Month. These categorisations enable salespeople to allocate their time more effectively and avoid missing out critical steps in the sales process. Pipeline Management is where the salesperson can track, and record sales opportunities along the sales funnel, including finding new leads, qualifying those leads, sending quotations, tracking progress and recording orders won (Zoltners et al., 2021). This tool can also generate quotations documents and send them directly to sales contacts, reducing time spent by salespeople on administrative tasks. Selecting the right technology for the right function and at the right time is important to achieving positive results.

"*We are in midst of the Fourth Industrial Revolution, born of the union of a host of new digital, biological, and physical technologies, which will be exponentially more transformative than its predecessors*" (Suzman, 2022:1). While the traditional SFA systems allow salespeople to gain tangible benefits such as obtaining customer information, product stock levels and recording customer activities, they can also help salespeople to develop intangible tasks such as the development of knowledge, refining of skills and generating creativity (Zoltners et al., 2021). However, automation can be a scary space for some because of the presumption that it could take away roles that will be replaced entirely by automation. The World Economic Forum (WEF) reported that a considerable number of traditional jobs could be replaced by automation and smarter machines including AI. By 2025, it is estimated that 85 million traditional jobs may have disappeared, but that 95 million new roles will have been created by the adoption of new technology-based roles, upskilling and reskilling roles (Jaeger, 2021; Kande and Sonmez, 2020). The McKinsey Global Institute estimated that up to 47% of salesperson's activities could potentially be automated (Chui, Manyika and Miremadi, 2016). However, it is also argued that many roles are irreplaceable by automation as AI does not provide the required empathy and interpersonal rapport that customers require (Efti, 2022). While SFA technically frees people from tedious, repetitive duties so they can devote more time to more crucial jobs that call for critical and creative thinking, we will need to understand the balance between too much work and a different type of work. There is a gap between innovation and the skills necessary to use those innovations successfully (Schwartz, 2022).

Långstedt (2021) explored the impact of automation on person-job fit and concluded that greater automation would reduce the fit with those employees who excel in performing administrative and simple tasks which could lead to job losses and a reduction in staff numbers. However, providing education or additional training in more complex tasks could help to mitigate some of these job losses. Consequently, how and when SFA systems are introduced should be a matter for consultation with the sales team. The sales team can also influence how and when technology applications are implemented by requesting organisational support with reorganisations, adequate training in new systems and facilitative leadership throughout the introduction of new automated systems. Some of this training can be effectively achieved through AI (Zoltners et al., 2021). The next generation of salespeople must adapt themselves to the new business environment and make efficient and effective usage of sales technologies by developing a new set of skills. Ease of use, effectiveness and system adaptability contribute significantly to the acceptance of SFAs (Mahlamäki et al., 2020). SFA systems have become a crucial part of a buyer-seller relationship, but it should be noted that no technology can fully replace a salesperson as they provide that unique, personalised service that can establish a rapport that helps them to understand the customers' needs so that they can help customers make complex decisions. The nature of the customer-supplier relationship revolves around commitment, trust and satisfaction. Based on past experiences, any emerging technology capable of improving any of these constructs will have a chance to find a place in the sales process (Singh et al., 2019).

Digitalisation changes both buying processes and sales processes but are perceived by customers as improving effectiveness and therefore enhancing the value of the sales interaction (Mahlamäki et al., 2020). A critical point is that many customers appreciate being offered a range of ways of interacting with the selling organisation. Digital platforms can replace many face-to-face sales interactions, especially for repeat or straight-forward orders, which allows for a better fit with the supply chain and greater efficiency in the sales process. Digital platforms also allow customers to learn about products online and place orders directly, which significantly reduces the travel time and time management costs of meeting salespeople face-to-face. Most customers will use general search engines, virtual trade shows, online expert opinion and organisational blogs, informational webpages and other online resources such as social media before engaging with salespeople (Mantrala and Albers, 2022). Consequently, potential customers may have made purchase decisions before meeting the salesperson, which could put the salesperson at a disadvantage in the negotiation. Those salespeople who use the power of technology to improve the selling processes by automating part of it, may be concerned that they are handing over control of the purchase decision-making processes to a computer and the customer (Cortez, Johnston and Dastidar, 2023). Resistance to new technologies is common as humans are inclined to react negatively to change and organisations can be slow to adopt digital systems. Several reasons for slow adoption have been proposed, from changing the scope of the project, being over ambitious and not providing sufficient training so that users do not get the benefits of the adoption (Zoltners et al., 2021). An additional problem for sales and marketing people is that they may feel that their personal time is being eroded by the constant need to engage with customers digitally outside working hours (Singh et al., 2019). Therefore, new SFA systems should be carefully selected so they are fit for purpose, communicate the benefits, and provide use-led training and mentoring for all relevant staff.

While the role that digital technology is mostly focused on the automation of routine tasks there is also a move towards automating the customer decision-making processes. The challenge of moving decision-making to computer systems are mainly ones of security and privacy. However, these risks can be mitigated by employing blockchains that are encrypted to make it much harder for information to accessed (Turi, 2020). Blockchain technology allows buyers and sellers to connect without a third-party or intermediaries being involved. This is a great leap forward in the customer-supplier relationship as it provides a much safer environment to transfer information and money between two parties using smart contracts. Smart contracts can resolve the issue of trust in a customer-supplier relationship (Tapscott and Tapscott, 2017). At the same time, employing this kind of technology means that sales operations can remain open, globally online, 24 hours a day, so that customers are able to place an order at any time they want to without the need to rely on a salesperson's availability. By applying automation tools, the organisation can also move towards paperless economy, making the company greener and meeting many B2B customer's expectations (Oliveira et al., 2021). Therefore, thorough constant adaptation to SFA technologies, organisations can bring a positive impact to the overall economy and the lives of people.

Big data analysis is another element in the digitalising world of sales as it has the potential to affect a company's entire operational environment. Big data refers to the amount of information gathered that cannot be analysed through traditional database tools because of the quantity of data involved (Anshari et al., 2019). Big Data Analysis (BDA), is a tool used in data mining (collection, storage and analysis) of large volumes of data and used widely to improve the accuracy of information and performance in sales (Shahbaz et al., 2021). BDA also enables multi-way communications, personalisation and customisation in the customer experience, which can be integrated with CRM systems and linked to marketing programs (Anshari et al., 2019). There are some challenges. With integrating BDA with CRM in terms of verifying data authenticity, and the legitimacy/safety of the data source especially if social media is used as a source. The application of Big Data analytics in sales is mostly focused on improving the customer journey and enhancing customer decision-making, where it can establish, sustain, and build the organisation's relationship with customers (Anshari et al., 2019).

Knowledge is crucial for a salesperson as they can target their communications with their customers in line with their needs. Algorithms, AI and machine learning (ML) are playing an increasing role in these activities. There are huge advantages for the salesperson where digital systems can provide knowledge management, control time efficiency, and increase the speed of decision making (Singh, Singh and Gupta, 2020). Big data can easily be processed by supercomputers to provide salespeople with clear leads to new customers, up-to-date customer knowledge, and market and stock information (Shahbaz et al., 2021). Supercomputers not only are able to analyse the ways in which decision-makers are going to make their decision but also provides valuable advice to the salespeople to make their choices more efficient and effective (Syam and Sharma, 2018). Hyper automation is a disciplined approach that orchestrates and harnesses the power of many technologies to provide end-to-end automation throughout the process. Hyper automation can guide the buyer to purchase in only 26 seconds (Gordon, 2022).

According to Vesal, Siahtiri and O'Cass (2021) a successful CRM system can improve a company's sales and market performance by maintaining customer relationships and tracking sales activities by analysing data and storing information, including contact information and accounts, in a centralised location. Cloud computing has been defined as "*a style of computing in which scalable and elastic IT-enabled capabilities are delivered as a service using Internet technologies*" (Bala et al., 2021:1). As a sales example, organisations can create algorithms that are used identically by a range of social media platforms to suggest possible sales solutions and services for its clients. This was made possible by software and a cloud computing system, that allows organisations to set up a network infrastructure connected to databases without the previously required physical hardware. Cloud Computing has significantly lowered the cost of sales force automation and allows scalable applications such as CRMs to be built. Cloud computing enables organisations to collect, store and analyse huge datasets that then inform the consistent and swift flow of information, customer lead generation, customer priorities, and market intelligence which has enabled sales teams to build and maintain customer relationships (Zoltners et al., 2021). The plasticity of cloud computing enables businesses to expand computing resources to match the needs of customers and scale back, therefore optimising costs and offering customers the best experience (Bala et al., 2021).

AI and AR

Selling through digital channels is becoming the norm for many organisations and using artificial intelligence tools allow selling organisations to interact with their customers through artificial intelligence bots (AI) that identify their requirements through needs recognition software and predict purchase patterns. The difference between SFA and AI is that AI refers to a group of technologies that provide machines with the social and cognitive abilities that are akin to human capabilities, but which are based on the analysis of data sets (Abbass, 2021). Simply, it is the work done by computers or software that formally required human intelligence to execute. AI in many ways is superior to how a human mind approaches a problem because it can analyse and process large amounts of data in seconds and recognise patterns to make judgements faster than humans (Chen and Zhou, 2022). Even though AI technologies are still in their infancy, their affects are already being felt. AI plays a significant role in the automation of sales processes through applications that can perform repetitive tasks (Hildebrand and Bergner, 2019). The number of companies that have implemented AI software has increased exponentially since 2015 (Chen and Zhou, 2022) and it is understood that AI is operating on the internet, in big data analysis, through cloud computing and other associated technologies.

AI has become the core technology for most selling activities online (Dennis and Yasin, 2021). The software provides many services such as pipeline generation, deal management, revenue forecasting and salesforce performance management. Three levels of AI have been described as Artificial Narrow Intelligence (ANI), Artificial General Intelligence (AGI) and Artificial Super Intelligence (ASI). According to Dennis and Yasin (2021), Narrow AI is developed for specific (narrow) tasks that cannot be easily integrated into other tasks, while the scope of AGI's is wider and it provides the adaptability that is intended to be equivalent to human capacity. ASI is the level that has the potential to exceed human intelligence and capabilities, such as processing and of analysing vast amounts of data. It is the narrow ANI software that currently provides considerable help and assistance for salespeople. When AI is further developed and reaches the AGI level, it will be possible for it to solve more complex problems with little or no human involvement (Syam and Sharma, 2018). The real-life implications of AGI software development could result in a technology that communicates with customers with consideration for their background, values and beliefs, leaving the salesperson to close the deal and follow up. In the post-purchase stage, ASI can provide the additional data that can provide insights into future purchasing behaviours.

Organisations are using intelligent communication tools (AI) to drive conversations with customers. Chatbots are used to communicate automatically with customers by replying to basic queries or solving general problems, without salespeople engagement. AI-powered chatbots help organisations to cut processing time and cost. When these issues are resolved quickly/immediately, the level of customer satisfaction increases. However, acceptance of AI requires that the salesperson and businesses trust that it is accurate, and that they can speak with a human if there are difficulties (Chen and Zhou, 2022). AI-powered contact centres provide solutions that improve customer interactions. As contact centre software can store all interaction data with customers, it allows salespeople to use those conversations such as emails, in extracting customers' insights (Latinovic and Chatterjee, 2022). In B2C selling, for example, WeChat (China's largest social networking platform), and Google can use AI systems to identify information about their customers buying behaviours as they use and communicate with each other through the platform. AI chatbots not only provide customers with immediate product information but can now sell unsupervised all day, every day (Hildebrand and Bergner, 2019).

AI is increasingly being used to analyse the needs of potential and existing customers to predict their future needs (Singh et al., 2019). Using algorithms, AI can easily track what a particular customer wants and then target a specific set of customers for a defined product range. The system can also analyse interactions during sales calls to scan the tone of the client to predict unmentioned issues and relay the information to the sales representative in real time (Singh et al., 2019). AI in sales has already started to outperform an average sales representative due to its predictive nature and accuracy. AI can help to target the customers precisely with a customised offer based on their buying behaviour and industry data. CRM systems can be integrated with AI to obtain customer data from various sources and use mathematical models to correlate input and output data to predict requirements (Li and Xu, 2022). This data may also be used by the sales team to create a picture of the customer to increase consumer value through sales personalisation and effectiveness (Rusthollkarhu, Hautamaki and Aarikka-Stenroos, 2020).

CRM systems can be integrated with AI systems to achieve similar levels of knowledge with B2B customers, which is changing the relationship between salespeople and customers as AI takes over some of the interactions, requiring salespeople to adopt to the technology to provide better solutions and alternative services to meet the growing needs of customers. A study showed that AI functions that were embedded within CRM systems was estimated to boost global business revenues by 1.1 trillion dollars from beginning of 2017 to the end of 2021 (Galitsky, 2020). Obviously, these digital tools can increase revenue for companies, while the overall customer experiences are also improved which drives them to repurchase the organisation's products and increase the customer lifetime value. AI can facilitate sales with B2B customers when they can communicate with organisations effectively. However, collecting customer data to power AI and CRM systems to deliver the quality of service, benefits and usability required to give confidence to customers, which should help them to interact with the system and provide their information accurately (Agnihotri et al., 2017). AI technology can also be used to interact with both existing and potential customers. CRM vendors have been making improvements to their CRM/AI functionalities so that they can understand and satisfy the customers' needs (Galitsky, 2020).

AI also powers humanoid robots that can answer questions about product information, read a customer's emotions and respond empathetically. Such applications will advance sales success, not just because customers' needs and demand for information will be exceeded, but also because these applications are entertaining (Hildebrand and Bergner, 2019). In the future, it may be possible to see retail robots in almost every store. These robots are used as information collectors. They can catch detailed information from shoppers about their purchasing behaviours as they move between items on the racks. All the observations will provide information on areas that will help the sales department in bringing out important focal points that will increase effectiveness and precision in stock management. Robots will even capture the facial recognitions of the buyers when they are viewing items on the racks and can even predict their next move. Additionally, Robots can walk through the retail premises taking pictures of the shelves and passageways that are then digitalised and turned into insights on pricing and information on merchandising to identify out-of-stock items (Forgan, 2020).

The rapid advancement in technology has encouraged sales organisations to find new ways of constantly adapting to dynamic market conditions. The newest technologies can also integrate and learn, scaling the automation, and marrying tools such as AI, ML and VR with robotic process automation (RPA), which automates work that people do repeatedly. The sales team is one among many that will be affected by the age of robots, and it involves using software to automate commercial operations, particularly those related to sales, such as managing data, responding to communications such as email and processing various transactions (Forgan, 2020; Långstedt, 2021). RPA also has the potential to contribute to the sales pipeline, facilitating both remote and hybrid working practices for sales and sales management (Paschen, Wilson and Ferreira, 2020). RPA has changed sales customer relations in several ways, through AI chatbots, humanoid sales robots, and vocal analysis to provide a better understanding of customers through customer interactions with the company's digital touch points. An organisation can use auto-bot lead engagement systems (chatbots) to engage with potential and existing customers through the purchasing process, handing customers onto other technology touchpoints such as webinars and e-sales as appropriate (Agnihotri et al., 2017; Sanfilippo, 2022).

Using Natural Language Processing (NLP) AI automate a lot of sales interactions through tools such as chatbots, autofill information, automated emails to customers, sales forecasting, calculating customer acquisition cost, voicemails and sales reports, through which sales organisations can understand the customers written or verbal response to their products or services. Once understood, these messages can then be communicated to the salesperson or manager. For example, if a customer sends a mail that includes the word 'urgent', NLP will pick up the word 'urgent' and prioritise that call to the right salesperson (Hansen, 2021). While personal selling has been the standard approach in the sales world for as long as sales have existed, newer sales technologies like AI, AR and VR are making leaps in the world of sales and quickly taking over human-to-human interaction. AI and ML have increased lead generation by 50% and reduced the costs by 40%–50% for the sales team today (Galitsky, 2020).

AI systems can also be aligned with AR and Virtual Reality (VR) systems to provide customer experience through digital platforms (Gordon, 2022). The use of these technologies can accelerate the consumer and customer decision-making processes as customers can experience and interact with virtual products online. The increase in online sales activities, may mean that organisations lose sales opportunities if they lack the technology to provide these facilities (Nguyen et al., 2022). As organisations continue to use automated-driven processes to meet customer expectations the systems will continue to collect relevant data that will be inputted into the management programme generating and facilitating ML. It is suggested that human-like AI will become a reality soon due to the exponential improvements in technological tools such as voice recognition, image recognition, deep learning and AI algorithms. As the ML system analyses data and respond appropriately to each customer in real-time without salespeople intervention it will increase the value for both parties, reducing costs and customising experiences (Rusthollkarhu, Hautamaki and Aarikka-Stenroos, 2020). However, management will need to pay attention to the balance between the cost of these new systems and their potential benefits. Anticipated cost savings from automation may not be realised if the system is too expensive or if it does not deliver as effectively as required. Further, there is the risk that an organisation becomes 'locked-into' a specific system that is either unable to keep up with their needs or suffers from price rises year on year (Keegan, Canhoto and Yen, 2022).

VR provides users with a different facility, that of interacting in the virtual environment with simulated objects which can create a unique atmosphere for the customer. AR provides users with both virtual and real objects in a real environment that can added value to customer interactions. Extended Reality (XR) according to a study by Fischer, Seidenstricker and Poeppelbuss (2021) can be used in several key applications in sales which are presentations, project planning, training and installation, and maintenance support. Arguably, most of the common in-person sales activities can be replaced with VR, AR and XR, although the costs may be prohibitive in some situations. These technologies are valuable when selling large/expensive/unique products such as medical equipment. AR can also be implemented in service-related industries such as education or tourism (Tan, Chandukala and Reddy, 2021). From a sales perspective, by providing an immersive, remote experience of a product or a service, customer satisfaction can be increased.

Engaging Through Social Media

All markets are facing significant changes due to increasing digitalisation of the sales process (Ancillai et al., 2019). In today's business environment salespeople are being driven to use technology to interact with customers and potential customers to provide services to their customers and partners (Ogilvie et al., 2018). Social selling is a relatively new idea that is becoming relevant to opening-up new opportunities that increase sales, and therefore companies need to be ready for these changes (Itani, Agnihotri and Dingus, 2017). Most companies have a lot of work to do to become a strong digital enterprise, but the speed of change is huge, and salespeople need to be adaptive. It took telephone companies 38 years to reach 50 million users last century, Facebook did it in two years (Rapp and Panagopoulos, 2012). As social selling becomes more commonplace, both sales and marketing people are required to build online relationships as well as physical ones. As these are frequently based in individual social media domains and interactions, they are demanding new resources and skills, which some existing salespeople are struggling to develop, and this is exacerbated by sales managers that are proving slow to recognise social media's potential (Cartwright, Liu and Raddats, 2021). Social selling is leveraging digital channels for understanding, connecting with and engaging prospects and existing customers at various parts of the buying process (Ancillai et al., 2019).

Social media is being used at every area of the sales process and can be utilised by sales professionals to generate content and engagement with the customers cognitive and emotional investment in the brand (Cartwright, Davies and Archer-Brown, 2021). Social media is an enabler for competitive intelligence collection and adaptive selling (Itani, Agnihotri and Dingus, 2017). Inbound sales are now reaching customers through multiple touch points and channels, such as websites, social media, emails, chatbots and apps to sell products and services without the need for salespeople to work face-to-face with customers (Mahlamäki et al., 2020). Social media platforms where people can interact with each other are estimated to provide information on products and services for more than 90% of purchases around the world (Arafah and Muhammad, 2022), so it is not surprising that the largest benefit from social media has been found to be from sales-facilitation, followed by integrated communications and employee engagement. It is a way to help potential customers perceive that an offer is valuable by interacting with user-generated content, either asynchronously or in real-time. Organisations that are building relationships with their customers need to recognise that social media platforms such as Facebook, LinkedIn, WeChat, TikTok and Twitter can be effectively utilised to contact a wider range of potential customers, and to create a deeper and more meaningful conversation with their existing customers through the communication of strong content and by selecting of the right channel (Cartwright, Davies and Archer-Brown, 2021).

It has been identified that salespeople were regularly using around 60 social media activities in their sales role, which demonstrates that one of social media's greatest potentials for salespeople is at the front-end of the sales cycle during the prospecting, lead qualification and pre-sales research that may ultimately lead up to a face-to-face meeting with the prospect (Ancillai et al., 2019). Referrals coming from LinkedIn, interests from blog sites, "likes" on Facebook, and large-scale analysis of Twitter information all benefit salespeople in developing new customers. Organisations can position themselves in the market through social media interactions on sites such as Twitter. The LinkedIn social selling index (SSI) indicates that social media is supplementing face-to-face engagements and developing relationships and networks (Cartwright, Liu and Raddats, 2021). When done effectively, social media interactions can create a narrative about the organisation's activities with their network that emphasises the role that they want to play in the market (Pardo, Pagani and Savinien, 2021). Continuing research into the use of social media to engage with customers has identified that one of the key messages is that the approach to SM implementation should be both coordinated and collaborative across the organisation. So even though salespeople are likely to be running their own interactions, their content needs to be aligned with the organisations' messages and resources, and targeted at selected audiences (Cartwright, Davies and Archer-Brown, 2021).

Building Online Customer Relationships

Participating on social media sites can help sales and marketing people to keep abreast of new ideas and themes and associate the selling organisation with specific topics (Cartwright, Davies and Archer-Brown, 2021).

Research has identified LinkedIn as one of the most effective social media platforms to use in sales and marketing (Cortez, Johnston and Dastidar, 2023). According to LinkedIn research, 89% of top sales professionals find social networking platforms such as LinkedIn important to closing deals (Rainsalestraining.com). The key is to find areas of common interest, concern or to provide links to informed figures within the industry. The salesperson can generate online conversations that are relevant to the buyer and establish a framework for their purchasing activities and be encouraged to move into buying activities through email blasts, landing page optimisations and live sales calls. Salespeople can decide what social communities to join that are relevant to their business, which can help them gain insights and engage digitally with prospects and customers (Cartwright, Davies and Archer-Brown, 2021; Chaker et al., 2022). Salespeople can also become an Internet 'friend' where they create a trustworthy persona that the customer will be willing to contact when they have a problem they need to solve. Once the potential customers are engaged, sales technology may be used to match customers with various sales processes that improves the organisation's visibility and generates conversations with designated sales and marketing people on relevant topics. This online alignment of sales and marketing activities can bring integration-based benefits to customer services especially where it delivers a 360-degree view of the customers' needs and meets jointly set KPIs (Corsaro, Maggioni and Olivieri, 2021).

Customers use search engines, attend virtual tradeshows, engage in specialist blogs and visit organisation's websites to ask questions or participate in discussions, often before they speak to a salesperson (or the organisation). Buyers are a lot more technically and digitally savvy and are spending more time on their devices researching products, offers and salespeople! It has been found that most buyers (82%) will review a salesperson's LinkedIn profile and form a judgement on them, before accepting a meeting or otherwise connecting directly with them. As much as eight out of every ten buyers are vetting salespeople on LinkedIn before deciding whether to respond (Cortez, Johnston and Dastidar, 2023; Sheahan, 2020). As a result of this online research, many buying decisions are made early in the process and buyers/customers are becoming more demanding since technology is giving them the tools to apply more leverage in their negotiations. As a result, they are looking to engage with salespeople in their own time, when they are available, and not necessarily in the seller's time (Chui, Manyika and Miremadi, 2016). Although salespeople can communicate information to customers more effectively and provide personalised customer interactions through the effective use of social media tools (Ogilvie et al., 2018), some customers and prospects will still require the human touch and salespeople may fear the loss of personal interaction with their existing customers that could create issues around trust and loyalty, which could have long term consequences to both sales and for future value creation (Cartwright, Davies and Archer-Brown, 2021).

There is a huge variation in the use of social media in selling inter-actions and many salespeople are still struggling to integrate social media into their activities. To mitigate some of these issues, managers should be leading by example by demonstrating their total commitment to adopting new, integrated working practices and providing online training for their team to help with the additional pressures that social media can create (Zoltners et al., 2021). Since inside salespeople do not have the opportunity to meet face-to-face with customers interacting through social media can bring significant benefits. These include learning about the prospects/customers and engaging with them (Chaker et al., 2022). One area that is helpful is training employees in the use of social media. Research has shown where companies offer formal social media training programs, sales has jumped from 28% to 74% in terms of adoption (Itani, Agnihotri and Dingus, 2017). Exploring how to engage with customers from a secure, closed training environment helps sales-people to experiment with creating social media interactions and avoiding some of the pitfalls of conversing online. Additionally, sales and marketing teams can be encouraged to use social media jointly and integrate new communication channels into their working practices (Cortez, Johnston and Dastidar, 2023). Sales and marketing people could also be offered social media mentors, which may also help with building stronger, cohesive teams by integrating traditional skills with the new opportunities offered by social media.

Organisations should be encouraged to take advantage of social media not only to gather valuable information about their customers and inte-grate that information into the CRM they are currently using, but also to engage in conversations and information exchanges to inform inbound sales thereby creating extended relationships online (Cartwright, Davies and Archer-Brown, 2021). When social media is combined with traditional CRM system it can improve customer-oriented processes, including modifying offers to meet customers' changing needs, measuring customer satisfaction, and connecting the needs of customers with sales activities (Agnihotri et al., 2017). For example, when prospecting for new cus-tomers, salespeople can make viral propositions, which is cost-effective but may have a lower customer conversion rate than the traditional pipeline. Salespeople can analyse the User Persona of different social media and adopt different marketing strategies depending on which platform they are engaged on. It has also been found that customers want to become value co-creators rather than passive buyers of new offers through social media interactions (Syam and Sharma, 2018). Social media interactions can therefore positively affect the performance of salespeople (Cortez, Johnston and Dastidar, 2023).

Conclusion

The more technology grows, the more controversial the topic is becoming for salespeople as they are required to adapt to online interactions whilst still retaining their traditional sales abilities. One of the most intriguing technology disruptions to sales is the mixture of augmented and VR. The metaverse, *"a collective virtual shared space, created by the convergence of virtually enhanced physical and digital reality"* (Gartner, 2022:1), could become a new sales channel where is it possible to create sales meetings, demonstrate products and provide training. There are many promising, innovative sales technologies that are emerging all the time, such as Multimodality (a combination of multiple sensory and communicative modes used in ML) or Generative AI (Dressman, 2019). Salespeople will have to become more adaptive and will require more digital literacy skills, data science, AI skills and training on virtual sales, while not compromising on their interpersonal skills.

AI "refers to programs, algorithms, systems and machines that demonstrate intelligence" (Shankar, 2018, p.vi). Therefore, AI and ML are married to provide real-time responses to customers without a salesperson's supervision. Although AI/ML are replacing some sales activities, but they are working at a much higher pace than people and increasing productivity. The main advantage of ML is that it can order large amounts of unstructured data whether is it text, images or numbers, in an integrated manner and it has a strong predictive performance (Ma and Sun, 2020). The system also can transfer learning to salespeople by being able to analyse patterns within AI interactions to predict or identify potential opportunities or challenges. One study used ML to identify why sales proposals were being rejected and from all the data identified that supplier failure often resulted from variation in contract valuation, how the product was presented, the proposal of ideas, past relationships, and managerial/staffing issues (Nguyen et al., 2022). These may not be surprising results and they have been proposed in previous literature, but the research highlighted why these were the key issues from the buyers' perspective, rather than looking at this issue from the sellers' perspective. Without the ML analysis this viewpoint would not have been discernible in the data.

AI interactions are a way of augmenting salespeople's skills, and it should always be remembered that a personal touch is beneficial because sales is all about giving a personalised customer experience and an over-dependency on technology can hinder performance. There is a 'productivity paradox' that states as technology advances, procedures become slower. This is because customers can spend considerable time accessing apps, switching between them, learning from them and engaging in other allied activities that may result in fewer sales. According to Galitsky (2020) in the future, robots and drones could substitute for humans, but even with increasing automation and the use of AI chatbots, a lot of people still want to talk to salespeople and discuss their problems as its easier to talk to a human than a chatbot. Consequently, there needs to be a healthy ratio of humans to technology. Having technology help salespeople will make the process easier but for now it is a better strategy to include people in the process of sales than automating the entire process.

References

Abbass, H. (2021). Editorial: What is artificial intelligence? *IEEE Transactions on Artificial Intelligence*, 2(2), 94–95. Available at: https://ieeexplore.ieee.org/stamp/stamp.jsp?tp=andarnumber=9523786. (Accessed: December 12, 2022).

Agnihotri, R., Trainor J, K., Itani, S. O., and Rodriguez, M. (2017). Examining the role of sales-based CRM technology and social media use on post-sales service behaviours in India. *Journal of Business Research*, 81, 144–154.

Ancillai, C., Terhob, H., Cardinalia, S., and Pascuccia, F. (2019). Advancing social media driven sales research: Establishing conceptual foundations for B-to-B social selling. *Industrial Marketing Management*, 82, 293–308.

Anshari, M., Almunawar, M. N., Lim, S. A., and Al-Mudimigh, A. (2019). Customer relationship management and big data enabled: Personalization and customization of services. *Applied Computing and Informatics*, 15(2), 94–101.

Arafah, B., and Muhammad, H. (2022). Social media as a gateway to information: Digital literacy on current issues in social media. *Webology*, 19(1), 2491–2503.

Bala, R., Gill, B, Smith, D, Wright, D., and Ji, K. (2021). Magic quadrant for cloud infrastructure and platform services. Available at: http://139.59.48.110/wp-content/uploads/2021/06/Gartner-Public-Cloud-2020.pdf. (Accessed: December 04, 2022).

Bishop, D. (2020). Task Management Guide for Success, Really Simple Systems. Available at: https://www.reallysimplesystems.com/blog/task-management/. (Accessed: November 28, 2022).

Cartwright, S., Davies, I., and Archer-Brown, C. (2021). Managing relationships on social media in business-to-business organisations. *Journal of Business Research*, 125, 120–134.

Cartwright, S., Liu, H., and Raddats, C. (2021). Strategic use of social media within business-to-business (B2B) marketing: A systematic literature review. *Industrial Marketing Management*, 97(8), 35–58.

Chaker, N. N., Nowlin, E. L., Pivonka, M. T., Itani, O. S., and Agnihotri, R. (2022). Inside sales social media use and its strategic implications for salesperson-customer digital engagement and performance. *Industrial Marketing Management*, 100, 127–144.

Chen, J., and Zhou, W. (2022). Drivers of salespeople's AI acceptance: What do managers think? *Journal of Personal Selling & Sales Management*, 42(2), 107–120.

Chui, M., Manyika, J., and Miremadi, M. (2016). Where machines could replace humans-and where they can't (yet). *McKinsey Quarterly*, July. Available at: https://www.mckinsey.com/~/media/mckinsey/business%20functions/mckinsey%20digital/our%20insights/where%20machines%20could%20replace%20humans%20and%20where%20they%20cant/where-machines-could-replace-humans-and-where-they-cant-yet.pdf. (Accessed: December 04, 2022).

Corsaro, D., Maggioni, I., and Olivieri, M. (2021). Sales and marketing automation in the post-Covid-19 scenario: Value drivers in B2B relationships. *Italian Journal of Marketing*, 2021(4), 371–392.

Cortez, R. M., Johnston, W. J., and Dastidar, A. G. (2023). Managing the content of LinkedIn posts: Influence on B2B customer engagement and sales? *Journal of Business Research*, 155, 113388.

Dennis, S., and Yasin, U. (2021). A Perceived Risk Perspective on Narrow Artificial Intelligence. *PACIS 2021 Proceedings*. [online] Available at: https://aisel.aisnet.org/pacis2021/44. (Accessed: November 04, 2022).

Dressman, M. (2019). Multimodality and language learning. The handbook of informal language learning. 39–55.

Efti, S. (2022). Will automation ever replace the role of a sales rep? The Close Sales Blog. The Close Sales Blog. Available at: https://blog.close.com/sales-automation/. (Accessed: November 06, 2022).

Fischer, H., Seidenstricker, S., and Poeppelbuss, J. (2021). *Human Interaction, Emerging Technologies and Future Applications IV*. Cham: Springer, 123–130.

Forgan, B. (2020). What robots can do for retail. *Harvard Business Review*. 1.

Galitsky B. (2020). *Artificial Intelligence for Customer Relationship Management; Keeping Customers Informed*. Cham: Springer.

Gartner (2022). What is a Metaverse? And Should You Be Buying In? Available at: https://www.gartner.com/en/articles/what-is-a-metaverse. (Accessed: December 05, 2022).

Gordon, C. (2022). *The Future of Sales and the Pervasiveness of Technology*. Forbes Magazine. Available at https://www.forbes.com/sites/cindygordon/2022/06/01/the-future-of-sales-and-the-pervasiveness-of-technology/?sh=51fed7681e21. (Accessed: November 25, 2022).

Hansen, L. (2021). Using natural language processing for marketing. Technology Advice. Available at: https://technologyadvice.com/blog/marketing/nlp-marketing/. (Accessed: October 03, 2022).

Harrison, E. D., and Hair, F. J. (2017). The use of technology in direct selling marketing channels: Digital avenues for dynamic growth. *Journal of Marketing Channels*, 24(1–2), 39–50.

Hildebrand, C., and Bergner, A. (2019.) AI-Driven sales automation: Using chatbots to boost sales. *NIM Marketing Intelligence Review*, 11(2), 36–41.

Hunter, G. K., and Perreault Jr, W. D. (2006). Sales technology orientation, information effectiveness, and sales performance. *Journal of Personal Selling and Sales Management*, 26(2), 95–113.

Itani, S. O., Agnihotri, R., and Dingus, R. (2017). Social media use in B2B sales and its impact on competitive intelligence collection and adaptive selling: Examining the role of learning orientation as an enabler. *Industrial Marketing Management*, 66, 64–79.

Jaeger, E. (2021). Jobs replaced by technology will be surpassed by the 'jobs of Tomorrow', Forbes. Forbes Magazine. Available at: https://www.forbes.com/sites/forbesbusinesscouncil/2021/11/24/jobs-replaced-bytechnology-will-be-surpassed-by-the-jobs-of-tomorrow/?sh=31d72c775811. (Accessed: November 06, 2022).

Kande, M., and Sonmez, M. (2020). *Don't Fear AI. It will Lead to Long-Term Job Growth.* World Economic Forum, October. Available at: https://www.weforum.org/agenda/2020/10/dont-fear-ai-it-will-lead-to-long-term-job-growth/. (Accessed: December 12, 2022).

Keegan, B. J., Canhoto, A. I., and Yen, D. A. (2022). Power negotiation on the tango dancefloor: The adoption of AI in B2B marketing. *Industrial Marketing Management*, 100, 36–48.

Långstedt, J. (2021). How will our values fit future work? An empirical exploration of basic values and susceptibility to automation. *Labour and Industry*, 31(2), 129–152,

Latinovic, Z., and Chatterjee, S. C. (2022). Achieving the promise of AI and ML in delivering economic and relational customer value in B2B. *Journal of Business Research*, 144, 966–974.

Li, F., and Xu, G. (2022). AI-driven customer relationship management for sustainable enterprise performance. *Sustainable Energy Technologies and Assessments*, 52, 102103.

Ma, L., and Sun, B. (2020). Machine learning and AI in marketing – Connecting computing power to human insights. *International Journal of Research in Marketing*, 37(3), 481–504.

Mahlamäki, T., Storbacka, K., Pylkkönen, S., and Ojala, M. (2020). Adoption of digital sales force automation tools in supply chain: Customers' acceptance of sales configurators. *Industrial Marketing Management*, 91, 162–173.

Mantrala, M. K., and Albers, S. (2022). *The impact of the internet on B2B sales force size and structure*. In: Lilien, G. L., Peterson, J. A., Wuyts, S. (eds) Handbook of Business-to-Business Marketing. Edward Elgar Publishing, Cheltenham.

Nguyen, P., Friend, S. B., Chase, K. S., and Johnson, J. S. (2022). Analyzing sales proposal rejections via machine learning. *Journal of Personal Selling & Sales Management*, 10.1080/08853134.2022.2067554.

Ogilvie, J., Agnihotri, R., Rapp, A., and Trainor, K. (2018). Social media technology use and salesperson performance: A two study examination of the role of salesperson behaviours, characteristics, and training. *Industrial Marketing Management*, 75, 55–65.

Oliveira, J., Azevedo, A., Ferreira, J. J., Gomes, S., and Lopes, J. M. (2021). An insight on B2B firms in the age of digitalization and paperless processes. *Sustainability*, 13(21), 11565.

Pardo, C., Pagani, M., and Savinien, J. (2021). The strategic role of social media in business-to-business contexts. *Industrial Marketing Management*, 101, 82–97.

Paschen, J., Wilson, M., and Ferreira, J. J. (2020). Collaborative intelligence: How human and artificial intelligence create value along the B2B sales funnel. *Business Horizons*, 63(3), 403–414.

Rapp, A., and Panagopoulos, N. G. (2012). Perspectives on personal selling and social media: Introduction to the special issue. *Journal of Personal Selling and Sales Management*, 32(3), 301–304.

Rusthollkarhu, S., Hautamaki, P., and Aarikka-Stenroos, L. (2020). Value (co-) creation in B2B sales ecosystems. *Journal of Business and Industrial Marketing*, 36(4), 590–598.

Sanfilippo, M. (2022). *What is sales force automation?* Business News Daily. Available at: https://www.businessnewsdaily.com/16028-sales-force-automation.html. (Accessed: November 11, 2022).

Schwartz, P. (2022). Digital Skills Crisis: Four in five UK workers say they are unequipped for the future of work, News and Insights. Available at: https://www.salesforce.com/uk/news/press-releases/2022/01/27/digital-skills-crisis-four-in-five-uk-workers-say-they-are-unequipped-for-the-future-of-work/. (Accessed: December 05, 2022).

Shahbaz, M., Gao, C., Zhai, L., Shahzad, F., Luqman, A., and Zahid, R. (2021). Impact of big data analytics on sales performance in pharmaceutical organisations: The role of customer relationship management capabilities. *PLoS One*, 16(4), e0250229.

Shankar, V. (2018). How Artificial Intelligence (AI) is Reshaping Retailing, *Journal of Retailing*, 94(4), vi–xi.

Sheahan, K. (2020). Developing and Empirically Testing a Sales Pipeline Execution Process Framework. PhD Thesis. Technological University, Dublin.

Singh, J., Flaherty, K., Sohi, R. S., Deeter-Schmelz, D., Habel, J., Le Meunier-FitzHugh, K., Malshe, A., Mullins, R., and Onyemah, V. (2019). Sales profession and professionals in the age of digitization and artificial intelligence technologies: Concepts, priorities, and questions. *Journal of Personal Selling and Sales Management*, 39(1), 2–22.

Singh, N., Singh, P., and Gupta, M. (2020). An inclusive survey on machine learning for CRM: A paradigm shift. *Decision*, 47(4), 447–457.

Suzman, J. (2022). *Work: A Deep History, from the Stone Age to the Age of Robots.* New York: Penguin Books.

Syam, N., and Sharma, A. (2018). Waiting for a sales renaissance in the fourth industrial revolution: Machine learning and artificial intelligence in sales research and practice. *Industrial Marketing Management*, 69, 135–146.

Tan, Y. C., Chandukala, S. R., and Reddy, S. K. (2021). Augmented reality in retail and its impact on sales. *Journal of Marketing*, 86(1), 48–66.

Tapscott, D., and Tapscott, A. (2017). How blockchain will change organisations. *MIT Sloan Management Review*, 58(2), 10–13.

Troncoso, D. J. (2022). *26 best sales automation software tools in 2022* (Free and paid), MarketSplash. MarketSplash. Available at: https://marketsplash.com/sales-automationtools/. (Accessed: November 25, 2022).

Turi, A. N. (2020). *Technologies for Modern Digital Entrepreneurship.* Berkley: Apress.

Vesal, M., Siahtiri, V., and O'Cass, A. (2021). Strengthening B2B brands by signalling environmental sustainability and managing customer relationships. *Industrial Marketing Management*, 92, 321–331.

Zoltners, A. A., Sinha, P., Sahay, D., Shastri, A., and Lorimer, S. E. (2021). Practical insights for sales force digitalization success. *Journal of Personal Selling & Sales Management*, 41(2), 87–102.

Index

Printed in the United States
by Baker & Taylor Publisher Services